Financing Public Education in an Era of Change

K. FORBIS JORDAN
TERESA S. LYONS

A Publication of the
PHI DELTA KAPPA
EDUCATIONAL FOUNDATION
Bloomington, Indiana

Cover design by Peg Caudell

Library of Congress Catalog Card Number 92-60500
ISBN 0-87367-457-X

Acknowledgements

Many persons have provided encouragement and ideas for this work. We thank Lowell C. Rose, executive director of Phi Delta Kappa, and Derek L. Burleson, editor of Special Publications, for their confidence and support. The authors especially wish to acknowledge the significant contributions of Mark Ebert and John Goertemiller to the manuscript. Ebert did the basic research and initial draft of Chapter 5 on the courts and school finance, and Goertemiller performed similar duties for Chapter 2 on demographic changes. Special recognition also is due John T. McDonough for his critical review, insightful comments, and encouragement. The critique of the manuscript by Susan Deaton and the Arizona State University Seminar on Educational Management resulted in many valuable changes. Special appreciation also is extended to Mary P. McKeown for her critical editorial comments, encouragement, and support.

K. Forbis Jordan,
Arizona State University

Teresa S. Lyons,
University of Nevada/Las Vegas
March 1992

Table of Contents

 **Preface**

In recent years diverse economic, social, and legal concerns have brought renewed attention to the problem of financing public schools. The major economic concerns include the need for an educated populace to compete successfully in the international marketplace and the increasing expenditures needed for education during a period of reduced economic growth. Social concerns arise from the changing demographics of the nation and how the public schools respond to these changes. Legal concerns focus on the fairness of the current school finance system relative to ensuring equity to both students and taxpayers and to providing adequate funding to meet the educational needs of all students.

In order to respond to the educational needs of students and school districts, states have devised very complex finance formulas. But regardless of these complexities, the essential school finance questions are relatively simple: 1) what or who to fund, 2) what amount to fund, 3) where to get the money, and 4) how to share the funding among different levels of government.

To answer these questions requires that we look at the context within which public schools function and at the demographic, political, economic, social, and legal factors influencing school financing. Demographic factors include the number and nature of students to be served as well as their educational needs. Political and economic factors include what should be the level of funding and how it is allocated to schools. Societal factors include community values about the importance of education and the public's attitude about supporting education. Legal factors include the court decisions dealing with issues of equity and adequacy in financing public schools. The challenge for policymakers is to take all these factors into consideration when developing a school finance system that provides an equitable and adequate educational program for all students.

1

This book is intended for both educators and the general public who want to know more about the financing of public education. The challenge for the authors has been to present the basic concepts and supporting information about school finance without becoming immersed in too many technical details. Chapter 1 provides the political and economic context for understanding public school finance and identifies some of the major policy issues that must be addressed. Chapter 2 provides an overview of demographic trends and their implications for financing public education. Chapter 3 addresses the values influencing state systems of school finance. Chapter 4 reviews current state systems for financing public education. Chapter 5 discusses both historical and current involvement of the courts on matters of school finance. Chapter 6 presents an overview of the taxation system used to finance schools, including information about funding from various levels of government. The final chapter addresses issues related to the future of school finance systems.

CHAPTER 1

The Context for
Public School Finance

The development and maintenance of public school finance systems is a complex process, requiring continuous monitoring and updating because of changing economic and demographic conditions. Public elementary and secondary education is a major enterprise and the dominant employer in many communities. One person in five either attends or is employed in the nation's public elementary and secondary schools. This 50-state educational delivery system serves more than 40 million students in about 15,000 districts that include more than 80,000 schools.

Expenditures for public elementary and secondary schools currently exceed $200 billion annually. Funding comes from a combination of local, state, and federal sources, with most of it coming from state and local tax revenues. These revenues support the day-to-day operation of schools and are the largest single item in the budgets of state and local governments. Federal funding represents only about 7% of the total budget for education, and most of it is targeted for special programs.

Methods of financing public schools vary among states, and spending levels per pupil differ both within and among states. However, two basic legal principles guide the financing of the public schools in the United States. First, financing public education is a state responsibility. There is no provision for — or even the mention of — "education" in the U.S. Constitution. Thus education is reserved to the states. Second, even though states provide education through local school districts, they have a responsibility to serve all children equally, regardless of the wealth of the district in which a child resides. Through their state constitutions and statutes, each state delegates responsibility for operating schools to local school districts. The exception is Hawaii, which operates as a single school district.

3

Provisions for financing public schools involve several interactive policy decisions: appropriation of funds by state legislatures, adoption of district budgets by local boards of education, and assessment and collection of county property taxes. These are state and local decisions. Often state efforts to provide equality in funding are thwarted because of the context of the local and state political environment in which school funding decisions are made.

In the political environment, legislators are confronted with competing demands from local school districts as well as from public agencies. These competing demands often result in decisions that are not made on a rational basis of cost effectiveness or on a basis of equity, which gives students equal access to educational services. Thus political expediency often leads legislators to make decisions resulting in short-term solutions rather than decisions that over the long term are more educationally and economically sound. It is within this context that governors and legislators must grapple to find ways to fund schools that are both adequate and equitable.

Concerns and Issues

Citizen interest in providing adequate funding for public schools is high. For the past several years, school finance has ranked among the top concerns expressed by respondents to the annual Phi Delta Kappa/Gallup Polls of the Public's Attitudes Toward the Public Schools (Elam et al. 1991). One of the public's concerns is producing an educated workforce in order for the United States to remain competitive in the international economy. Another is the changes occurring in the family, which have led to increasing expectations of the schools. For example, interest in extended-day programs in schools has increased because of the increasing number of single-parent households and latch-key children. However, even this heightened interest may not be sufficient to generate public support for adequate funds to provide quality education. Providing adequate financing for public schools is becoming increasingly difficult because of a series of interactive social and economic developments.

The great debate of the 1990s may be over the proportion of funds spent for special-needs students versus funds needed for educating regular students or for other social services. In addition to the need for more funds to support education for all youth, competition for scarce public funds will come from the elderly living on fixed incomes, who need a variety of social services including better health care. Reconciling the needs of these competing groups will be a formidable challenge to policymakers.

Another issue is the extent to which the state school finance program should reduce the disparities in educational opportunity among districts and move toward providing an adequately funded program that is equitable for all pupils. However, equity and adequacy are not the only school finance goals. Local school officials want predictable and relatively stable levels of funding in order to facilitate orderly budgetary and educational planning. And they seek a financing system that responds to changing economic and demographic conditions. As the number of pupils increases and as costs for services and materials increase, there should be a commensurate increase in funding. Taxpayers also desire predictability and stability in their tax rates so that they can plan their fiscal affairs.

Other concerns are expressed about accountability of the schools. Some have advocated that funding for schools be based on pupil performance. However, under such a policy — and without stability in funding — underachieving school districts would have even less to spend, even though their needs might be greater.

Given the projected enrollment growth in urban areas, adequate funding for education becomes even more complex. Many of the nation's large cities face a declining tax base, an aging infrastructure, deterioration of social services, and expanding social needs. Even though social needs are increasing in urban areas, relief is unlikely, because the majority coalition in many state legislatures represents mostly suburban and rural interests. In addition, some states, such as California and Massachusetts, have enacted tax limitation legislation that severely restricts any increased funding for education.

Court Challenges

Legal challenges to state school finance systems also have brought increased public attention to the issue of funding public schools. These challenges focus on the wide variations in per-pupil spending among school districts within a state, resulting in unequal educational opportunity. These legal challenges have occurred in Alabama, Idaho, Illinois, Minnesota, Missouri, Ohio, Oklahoma, Pennsylvania, and Virginia. Moreover, the existing school financing systems have been declared unconstitutional in Montana, Texas, Tennessee, Kentucky, and New Jersey.

In the 1970s there was considerable interest in the legal aspects of school finance as a result of the U.S. Supreme Court's 5 to 4 decision in the *Rodriguez* case. (See Chapter 5 for a discussion of this important case.) Then, the legal concerns were related to equal treatment of students; today the focus is on equal access to educational opportunity.

After *Rodriguez*, litigation was initiated in several states; and state-level study commissions proliferated. State legislators were searching for ways to prevent the federal courts from taking action relative to school finance as they had done to desegregate the schools. The focus on school finance shifted to the provisions of each state's constitution and was followed by successful litigation in California, New Jersey, Washington, and West Virginia.

The quest for perfection in state school finance systems has resulted in an array of adjustments and restrictions designed to address special problems; these actions have made the systems extremely complex. Perhaps policymakers will come to the realization that the goal of enacting the perfect school finance system will never be attained. The great debate may be whether school finance reform leading to both adequacy and equity in funding can best be achieved through incremental improvements or through bold, revolutionary actions.

Education — An Expense or an Investment?

One of the continuing questions about financing schools, or any public service for that matter, is whether it should be viewed as a public expense or a societal investment. The general consensus among educators is that adequate funding for a quality education should be viewed as an investment in the future of the nation; whereas the failure of a nation to educate its populace results in a true expense — for both society and individuals. The Committee for Economic Development (1987) estimated that each year's class of dropouts will cost the nation $240 billion in lost earnings and foregone taxes over their lifetime. This projection does not include the billions more spent for crime control, welfare, health care, and other social services that will be required by this under-educated group.

Without adequate school funding, there is the potential for severe problems in those states projected to have major enrollment increases in students who are educationally disadvantaged because of limited English proficiency and poverty. Educational interventions to address these problems not only can increase the productivity of disadvantaged youth but also have the potential for reducing the costs for welfare and crime control.

A quality education for these special-needs populations requires lower pupil-teacher ratios and special instructional methods and materials. The Committee for Economic Development (1987) recognized that the needs of these special populations cannot be addressed simply by reallocation and more efficient use of current resources. The committee stated that any plan for improving the education of disadvantaged youth is doomed to failure if it does not recognize the need for additional resources over a sustained period. Business interests also have become interested in improving the quality of America's educational system, because a well-educated work force is essential for maintaining and improving the nation's competitive position in the international marketplace. Workers will have the income to purchase consumer goods, thus supporting the economy. In addition, these workers will need to be literate in order to make informed choices as citizens.

The interaction of legal, philosophical, and economic concerns has raised many questions about the fairness and responsiveness of the current educational system, questions that underlie much of the current interest in school finance reform. These questions were the impetus for the authors to write this monograph.

References

Committee for Economic Development. *Children in Need: Investment Strategies for the Educationally Disadvantaged.* New York, 1987.
Elam, S.M., et al. "The 23rd Annual Gallup Poll of the Public's Attitudes Toward the Public Schools." *Phi Delta Kappan* 73 (September 1991): 41-56.

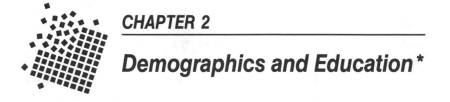

CHAPTER 2

*Demographics and Education**

A basic consideration in understanding public school financing is the impact of demographic factors on the educational enterprise. Such factors include the increases and decreases in enrollment, the mobility of students and families, and the changing nature of the students who attend school. This chapter will examine recent demographic developments and discuss their implications for financing education.

Population projections should be viewed with caution, because they assume predictable rates of growth among various population groups. But human beings often act in unpredictable and unexpected ways as a result of political and economic shifts and social developments. The accuracy of projections is affected by changing fertility rates, by immigration statutes and regulations made by Congress and the U.S. Immigration and Naturalization Service, and by the different values held by various racial, ethnic, and even religious groups. Other factors affecting projections include increased longevity attributable to improvements in health care and fluctuations in the economy influencing family planning decisions.

The Current Demographic Picture

According to the Bureau of the Census, the total population of the United States as of 1 April 1990 was in excess of 248.7 million, with an average of 70.3 people per square mile. Since the preceding decennial census in 1980, the increase was more than 22 million, or an increase of 9.8%. This rate of growth has been fairly steady. For example, the estimated net increase in 1991 was approximately two

---

*The basic research for and initial draft of this chapter were done by John Goertemiller, research assistant in the Department of Educational Administration and Higher Education, University of Nevada/Las Vegas.

8

million. With natural attrition through death, this increase represents more than four million new persons — new consumers of goods, services, and resources and new consumers of education.

Even though the population continues to grow, the rate of increase has declined in each 10-year period since the 1960 census. The 1960 census indicated a rather high rate of increase (18.4%) over the previous decade. Since then the rates have decreased by several percentage points each decade. (See Table 2.1.)

Table 2.1. Total United States population and increase.

Census	Population	Increase Over Preceding Census	
		Number	Percent
1950	151,325,798	19,161,229	14.5
1960	179,323,175	27,997,377	18.4
1970	203,302,031	23,978,856	13.4
1980	226,545,805	23,243,774	11.4
1990	248,709,873	22,164,068	9.8

Source: U.S. Bureau of the Census, 1991.

The bulge in the rate of growth that peaked in the 1960 census reflects the near completion of the effect of the Baby Boom generation, those born during the period 1946 through 1961. This population of 76 million represents the largest generation in U.S. history. Most of the children of this Baby Boom generation will have completed their elementary and secondary schooling by the year 2000.

For purposes of educational planning, the population growth in the decade of the 1980s needs to be broken down by states and geographic region. By no means was the 22.2 million population increase and the 9.8% rate increase in this decade uniform across the states or geographic regions. States in the South and the West grew by 13.4% and 22.3% respectively. By contrast, the states in the Midwest and Northeast grew by a modest 1.4% and 3.4% respectively. (See Table 2.2.)

Since 1950, 40% of the total U.S. population growth has been in just three states: California, Florida, and Texas. Although the growth rate in Texas slowed in the decade of the 1980s due to adverse economic conditions resulting from the decline in oil prices, the population in California alone grew by approximately six million, more than half of whom were immigrants from outside the United States. Harold Hodgkinson (1986) points out that nearly two-thirds of the world's immigration is into the United States, and one-half of that is into the state of California. This development will put pressure on that state's political structure and affect the allocation of resources for education in the 21st century. Detailed immigration statistics are provided in Table 2.3.

Table 2.2. Immigrants admitted, by leading states of intended residence and country of birth: 1989 (in thousands).

Origin	Total	CA	NY	TX	IL	FL
Total	1090.0	457.4	134.8	112.9	69.3	48.5
Europe	82.9	16.1	15.8	2.2	9.6	4.1
Asia	312.1	119.3	39.5	14.5	15.4	6.8
China	32.3	11.1	10.6	0.9	0.9	0.5
Taiwan	13.9	6.0	2.0	0.9	0.4	0.2
India	31.1	5.6	4.6	1.9	3.3	0.9
Iran	21.2	11.6	1.4	1.3	0.5	0.6
Korea	34.2	10.6	4.3	1.4	1.7	0.5
Laos	12.5	5.5	0.3	0.4	0.3	0.1
Pakistan	8.0	1.4	1.6	0.8	1.1	0.4
Philippines	57.0	28.4	3.4	1.6	3.5	1.2
Thailand	9.3	4.4	0.4	0.4	0.4	0.2
Vietnam	37.7	16.0	1.5	2.8	0.8	0.8
North America	607.4	307.7	54.6	91.8	41.6	28.7
Canada	12.2	2.3	1.1	0.5	0.3	2.0
Mexico	405.2	244.8	1.8	81.5	37.8	2.8
Caribbean	88.9	1.7	43.1	0.7	0.8	17.2
Central America	101.0	58.8	8.5	9.1	2.7	6.7
South America	58.9	8.3	20.7	1.9	1.7	8.0
Africa	25.2	4.0	4.0	2.3	0.8	0.8
Other	4.4	2.1	0.2	0.2	0.1	0.1

Source: U.S. Immigration and Naturalization Service, *Statistical Yearbook*, 1990. This is an extract of data and does not identify all immigrant groups specifically.

Table 2.3. Immigrants admitted and major metropolitan areas of residence: 1989.

Metropolitan Area	Total Immigration	Largest Group (in thousands)
Los Angeles/Long Beach	262,805	Mexico (149.8)
New York	116,597	Caribbean (27.9)
Chicago	60,336	Mexico (32.5)
Anaheim/Santa Ana	36,597	Mexico (19.8)
Houston	34,682	Mexico (18.4)
Washington, D.C., Area	26,695	Central America (4.4)
Miami	24,569	Caribbean (2.8)
San Diego	23,233	Mexico (13.8)
San Francisco	22,754	México (3.8)
Riverside/San Bernardino	20,630	Mexico (14.7)
San Jose	19,891	Mexico (7.3)
Boston Area	17,160	China (1.3)
Oakland	15,843	Mexico (3.7)
Dallas	15,601	Mexico (9.5)

Source: U.S. Immigration and Naturalization Service, *Statistical Yearbook*, 1990. This is an extract of data and does not identify all immigrant groups for each metropolitan area. This table does not attempt to identify the areas with the same statistical terminology used by the INS.

As shown in Table 2.3, the distribution of new immigrants tends to be concentrated in a limited number of population centers. For example, of the Mexican immigrants in 1989 (405,000), 68% settled in the 10 largest metropolitan areas and are concentrated in the largest metropolitan areas of California. In contrast, the Vietnamese population, while significantly smaller at about 38,000, chose a more diverse set of locations. Only 58% settled in the 14 major metropolitan areas of the United States. This tendency to concentrate varies greatly among the different ethnic immigrant groups.

The impact of immigration likely will become greater with implementation of the 1990 Immigration Reform Act, which went into effect in October 1991. This legislation permitted immigration to increase from 540,000 to 700,000 persons per year. Also, "diversity" programs under the Immigration Reform Act will allot 40,000 Green Cards by lottery over the next three years.

Today, the major ethnic immigrant groups are concentrated in different regions of the United States. Hispanics (45%) are concentrated in the West, and 55% of Asians now live in the West. The growth rate is largest among these two ethnic groups, with the rate more than doubling between 1980 and 1990. This development will have long-term implications for the ethnic makeup of western metropolitan areas and for the public schools in those areas.

Of the black population, 54% live in the South. Although less than Hispanics and Asians, the growth rate for this ethnic group (13.2%) is significantly higher for the decade than the national average (Frey 1991).

Overall, the growth of minority groups has been a major factor in the 9.8% national growth rate in population during the 1980s. The white growth rate was only 4.4% in the same decade, but the overall minority growth rate was 30.9%. Only in the West was white growth rate (11%) in excess of the national average. However, the growth rate in the West in the past decade for minority populations was 53.4%. A summary of population distribution in 1990 by ethnic background is provided in Table 2.4.

The most dramatic changes occurred in the metropolitan areas where minorities tend to be concentrated. Asians (73%), Hispanics (69%), and blacks (58%) live in the large metropolitan areas, while less than half (46%) of the whites do.

Total enrollment in public and private elementary and secondary schools peaked at 51.3 million in 1971, with public school enrollment at 46 million. After this high point, due largely to the Baby Boom generation, public and private school enrollments declined steadily until 1984 when they were 44.9 million, with public school enrollment at 39.2 million. From 1984 to 1990, enrollment in public school grades K-8 rose modestly from 26.9 million to 29.5 million, whereas enrollment in grades 9-12 continued declining from 12.3 million to 11.3 million. By 1990 the overall public and private elementary and the secondary public school enrollment reached 46.2 million. (See Table 2.5.)

Private schools enrolled approximately 12% of the total school population. In 1990, private school enrollment was estimated at 4.2 million at the elementary level and 1.2 million at the secondary level. (See Table 2.5.) Enrollment projections indicate that the elementary and secondary school population will peak in 1998 at near the 1971 level followed by another period of gradual decline.

Table 2.4. Resident population, by race and Hispanic origin: 1990.

REGION AND STATE	NUMBER (in thousands)						PERCENT DISTRIBUTION				
	Total[1]	White	Black	American Indian Eskimo Aleut	Asian, Pacific Islander	Hispanic origin[2]	White	Black	American Indian Eskimo Aleut	Asian, Pacific Islander	Hispanic origin
U.S.	248,710	199,686	29,986	1,959	7,274	22,354	80.3	12.1	0.8	2.9	9.0
Northeast . . .	50,809	42,069	5,613	125	1,335	3,754	82.8	11.0	0.2	2.6	7.4
ME	1,228	1,208	5	6	7	7	98.4	0.4	0.5	0.5	0.6
NH	1,109	1,087	7	2	9	11	98.0	0.6	0.2	0.8	1.0
VT	563	555	2	2	3	4	98.6	0.3	0.3	0.6	0.7
MA	6,016	5,405	300	12	143	288	89.8	5.0	0.2	2.4	4.8
RI.	1,003	917	39	4	18	46	91.4	3.9	0.4	1.8	4.6
CT	3,287	2,859	274	7	51	213	87.0	8.3	0.2	1.5	6.5
NY	17,990	13,385	2,859	63	694	2,214	74.4	15.9	0.3	3.9	12.3
NJ	7,730	6,130	1,037	15	273	740	79.3	13.4	0.2	3.5	9.6
PA	11,882	10,520	1,090	15	137	232	88.5	9.2	0.1	1.2	2.0
Midwest	59,669	52,018	5,716	338	768	1,727	87.2	9.6	0.6	1.3	2.9
OH	10,847	9,522	1,155	20	91	140	87.8	10.6	0.2	0.8	1.3
IN	5,544	5,021	432	13	38	99	90.6	7.8	0.2	0.7	1.8
IL.	11,431	8,953	1,694	22	285	904	78.3	14.8	0.2	2.5	7.9
MI	9,295	7,756	1,292	56	105	202	83.4	13.9	0.6	1.1	2.2
WI	4,892	4,513	245	39	54	93	92.2	5.0	0.8	1.1	1.9
MN	4,375	4,130	95	50	78	54	94.4	2.2	1.1	1.8	1.2
IA.	2,777	2,683	48	7	25	33	96.6	1.7	0.3	0.9	1.2
MO	5,117	4,486	548	20	41	62	87.7	10.7	0.4	0.8	1.2
ND	639	604	4	26	3	5	94.6	0.6	4.1	0.5	0.7
SD	696	638	3	51	3	5	91.6	0.5	7.3	0.4	0.8
NE	1,578	1,481	57	12	12	37	93.8	3.6	0.8	0.8	2.3
KS	2,478	2,232	143	22	32	94	90.1	5.8	0.9	1.3	3.8
South	85,446	65,582	15,829	563	1,122	6,767	76.8	18.5	0.7	1.3	7.9
DE	666	535	112	2	9	16	80.3	16.9	0.3	1.4	2.4
MD	4,781	3,394	1,190	13	140	125	71.0	24.9	0.3	2.9	2.6
DC.	607	180	400	1	11	33	29.6	65.8	0.2	1.8	5.4
VA	6,187	4,792	1,163	15	159	160	77.4	18.8	0.2	2.6	2.6
WV	1,793	1,726	56	2	7	8	96.2	3.1	0.1	0.4	0.5
NC.	6,629	5,008	1,456	80	52	77	75.6	22.0	1.2	0.8	1.2
SC	3,487	2,407	1,040	8	22	31	69.0	29.8	0.2	0.6	0.9
GA	6,478	4,600	1,747	13	76	109	71.0	27.0	0.2	1.2	1.7
FL	12,938	10,749	1,760	36	154	1,574	83.1	13.6	0.3	1.2	12.2
KY	3,685	3,392	263	6	18	22	92.0	7.1	0.2	0.5	0.6
TN	4,877	4,048	778	10	32	33	83.0	16.0	0.2	0.7	0.7
AL	4,041	2,976	1,021	17	22	25	73.6	25.3	0.4	0.5	0.6
MS.	2,573	1,633	915	9	13	16	63.5	35.6	0.3	0.5	0.6
AR	2,351	1,945	374	13	13	20	82.7	15.9	0.5	0.5	0.8
LA	4,220	2,839	1,299	19	41	93	67.3	30.8	0.4	1.0	2.2
OK.	3,146	2,584	234	252	34	86	82.1	7.4	8.0	1.1	2.7
TX	16,987	12,775	2,022	66	319	4,340	75.2	11.9	0.4	1.9	25.5
West	52,786	40,017	2,828	933	4,048	10,106	75.8	5.4	1.8	7.7	19.1
MT	799	741	2	48	4	12	92.7	0.3	6.0	0.5	1.5
ID	1,007	950	3	14	9	53	94.4	0.3	1.4	0.9	5.3
WY	454	427	4	9	3	26	94.2	0.8	2.1	0.6	5.7
CO.	3,294	2,905	133	28	60	424	88.2	4.0	0.8	1.8	12.9
NM	1,515	1,146	30	134	14	579	75.6	2.0	8.9	0.9	38.2
AZ	3,665	2,963	111	204	55	688	80.8	3.0	5.6	1.5	18.8
UT	1,723	1,616	12	24	33	85	93.8	0.7	14	1.9	4.9
NV	1,202	1,013	79	20	38	124	84.3	6.6	1.6	3.2	10.4
WA	4,867	4,309	150	81	211	215	88.5	3.1	1.7	4.3	4.4
OR.	2,842	2,637	46	38	69	113	92.8	1.6	1.4	2.4	4.0
CA	29,760	20,524	2,209	242	2,846	7,688	69.0	7.4	0.8	9.6	25.8
AK	550	415	22	86	20	18	75.5	4.1	15.6	3.6	3.2
HI	1,108	370	27	5	685	81	33.4	2.5	0.5	61.8	7.3

Source: U.S. Bureau of the Census, press release CB91-100.

[1]Includes other races, not shown separately.

[2]Persons of Hispanic origin may be of any race.

13

Table 2.5. Enrollment in K-12, by level and control: 1950 to 2001 (in thousands).

Year	Total elementary and secondary	Public elementary and secondary schools			Private elementary and secondary schools		
		Total	K-8	9-12	Total	K-8	9-12
1950	28,492	25,111	19,387	5,725	3,380	2,708	672
1959	40,857	35,182	26,911	8,271	5,675	4,640	1,035
1964	47,716	41,416	30,025	11,391	6,300	5,000	1,300
1965	48,473	42,173	30,563	11,610	6,300	4,900	1,400
1966	49,239	43,039	31,145	11,894	6,200	4,800	1,400
1967	49,891	43,891	31,641	12,250	6,000	4,600	1,400
1968	50,744	44,944	32,226	12,718	5,800	4,400	1,400
1969	51,119	45,619	32,597	13,022	5,500	4,200	1,300
1970	51,272	45,909	32,577	13,332	5,363	4,052	1,311
1971	51,281	46,081	32,265	13,816	5,200	3,900	1,300
1972	50,744	45,744	31,831	13,913	5,000	3,700	1,300
1973	50,429	45,429	31,353	14,077	5,000	3,700	1,300
1974	50,053	45,053	30,921	14,132	5,000	3,700	1,300
1975	49,791	44,791	30,487	14,304	5,000	3,700	1,300
1976	49,484	44,317	30,006	14,311	5,167	3,825	1,342
1977	48,717	43,577	29,336	14,240	5,140	3,797	1,343
1978	47,636	42,550	28,328	14,223	5,086	3,732	1,353
1979	46,645	41,645	27,931	13,714	5,000	3,700	1,300
1980	46,249	40,918	27,677	13,242	5,331	3,992	1,339
1981	45,522	40,022	27,270	12,752	5,500	4,100	1,400
1982	45,166	39,566	27,158	12,407	5,600	4,200	1,400
1983	44,967	39,252	26,979	12,274	5,715	4,315	1,400
1984	44,908	39,208	26,901	12,308	5,700	4,300	1,400
1985	44,979	39,422	27,030	12,392	5,557	4,195	1,362
1986	45,205	39,753	27,419	12,334	5,452	4,116	1,336
1987	45,487	40,008	27,930	12,078	5,479	4,232	1,247
1988	45,433	40,192	28,501	11,692	5,241	4,036	1,206
1989	45,963	40,608	29,147	11,461	5,355	4,162	1,193
1990	46,192	40,801	29,546	11,255	5,391	4,219	1,172
1991	46,856	41,387	30,006	11,381	5,469	4,285	1,185
1992	47,546	41,997	30,423	11,574	5,549	4,344	1,205
1993	48,226	42,602	30,732	11,870	5,624	4,388	1,236
1994	48,909	43,214	30,930	12,284	5,695	4,417	1,279
1995	49,431	43,682	31,061	12,621	5,749	4,435	1,314
1996	49,843	44,054	31,104	12,950	5,789	4,441	1,348
1997	50,080	44,269	31,094	13,175	5,811	4,440	1,371
1998	50,136	44,319	31,098	13,221	5,817	4,441	1,376
1999	50,108	44,299	30,939	13,360	5,809	4,418	1,391
2000	49,976	44,186	30,754	13,432	5,790	4,391	1,398
2001	49,786	44,022	30,528	13,494	5,764	4,359	1,405

Source: U.S. Department of Education, National Center for Education Statistics, 1990.

Future Projections

Planning for the future will require more than understanding and interpreting current statistical and demographic data. Additional detailed information will be required for intelligent policy decisions. Commencing in the mid-1990s, the U.S. population growth rate will be at its lowest level ever. However, the problems confronting education will be complicated by several changes in the demographic characteristics, which will have a significant impact after the turn of the century.

Specifically, projections indicate that the total number of births and the number of white births will drop sharply during the next decade, a result of fewer women of childbearing age as the Baby Boom generation ages. However, black and other minority groups will grow at a much higher rate. By 2030 or 2040, it is projected that the black population will grow by another 50% (14 million); and the Asian/Pacific Islander/American Indian group will grow by a dramatic 300% (16 million). In addition, the U.S. population at the start of the 21st century will include the 9 million or so immigrants and their offspring who will have entered the country since 1989-1990. What seems clear is that a significant number of minority and immigrant children will be in our schools by the year 2000.

Projections from the U.S. Bureau of the Census (Current Population Reports, Series P-25, No. 1018) indicate that the U.S. population will reach 260.1 million in 1995 and 268.3 million by the year 2000. Longer-term projections indicate that a peak of approximately 302 million could be reached by 2040, followed by a gradual decline.

Another trend over the next several decades is the general aging of the population. The median age is projected to increase by one to two years per decade. In 1960 the median age was 29.4 years. In 1990 it was 33.0. By 2000 demographers project that it will be 36.4 years.

In the year 2000 the two population bulges will be in the 35-44 year age group and the 5-19 school-age group. At a point when the population is generally aging, the second largest population group will be those attending elementary and secondary schools. This bulge will occur when recruitment of new teachers will have to come from the relatively smaller 20-34 year age group. At the same time, much of the current teacher population will be preparing to retire.

For the past several years, the National Center for Education Statistics has reported that the number of public school teachers has risen at a rate faster than the number of students. (See Table 2.6.) When feasible, school districts took advantage of this availability of teachers and reduced their student-teacher ratios. In public schools in 1989, the average was 17.2 pupils per teacher, a decline from 19.1 pupils per teacher in 1979. Private schools reflect this trend even more strongly, dropping from 18.1 to 14.2 pupils per teacher in the same period. If this trend for lower pupil-teacher ratios continues, recruitment of teachers will be a priority among policymakers (U.S. Department of Education 1991).

The decline in students and the over-supply of teachers in the 1970s and 1980s enabled policymakers to limit salary increases and other benefits. This may have had a negative impact by deterring the best and brightest college students from pursuing a career in education. Certainly the supply and quality of teachers will be a crucial issue as the nation approaches the 21st century, and competitive salaries and other benefits will be a factor in recruiting good candidates to the profession.

These recruitment efforts will create pressures for additional funds for education. In 1990 expenditures for public and private elementary and secondary education totaled $215.5 billion, or approximately 7% of the Gross National Product. These data are important from two perspectives. First, to some extent, trends in per-pupil expendi-

Table 2.6. Teachers in elementary and secondary schools by control of institution: 1970 to 2000 (in thousands).

Level and type of control	1970	1975	1980	1985	1990*	1995*	2000*
Elementary and secondary teachers	2,288	2,451	2,485	2,550	2,785	3,016	3,212
Public schools	2,055	2,196	2,184	2,207	2,401	2,602	2,772
Private schools	233	255	301	343	384	414	439
Elementary teachers	1,281	1,352	1,401	1,483	1,642	1,751	1,848
Public schools	1,128	1,180	1,189	1,237	1,361	1,451	1,532
Private schools	153	172	212	246	281	300	316
Secondary teachers	1,007	1,099	1,084	1,067	1,142	1,266	1,364
Public schools	927	1,016	995	970	1,039	1,151	1,241
Private schools	80	83	89	97	103	114	123

Source: U.S. Department of Education, July 1990.
*Projected figures.

tures and teacher salaries over time are reflective of the nature of the nation's long-term commitment to education. Second, the trends will influence students in making the decision to enter the teaching profession. Table 2.7 summarizes these data in aggregate form. These data are national averages and serve as a general indicator.

Table 2.7. Expenditures and teacher salaries: 1976 to 2001 (figures in constant 1989 dollars).

Year	Expenditures ($ Billion)	$ Per Pupil Enrolled	Average Salary
1976	$135.7	$3,030	$27,555
1977	138.1	3,116	27,584
1978	141.5	3,241	27,493
1979	139.8	3,284	26,609
1980	135.9	3,264	24,955
1981	132.1	3,227	24,703
1982	130.2	3,254	24,829
1983	133.8	3,381	25,566
1984	137.5	3,502	26,114
1985	144.8	3,693	27,044
1986	152.8	3,875	28,061
1987	159.4	4,011	28,938
1988	164.5	4,112	29,305
1989	168.6	4,194	29,567
1990	174.4	4,295	30,145
1991	178.3	4,371	30,629
1992	184.4	4,456	31,106
1993	190.1	4,525	31,821
1994	195.9	4,598	32,513
1995	202.4	4,683	33,076
1996	209.0	4,784	33,654
1997	215.2	4,884	34,079
1998	221.1	4,995	34,462
1999	226.8	5,118	34,822
2000	232.4	5,245	35,142
2001	237.7	5,381	35,541

Source: U.S. Department of Education, National Center for Education Statistics, 1990. Projections through 2001 are based on middle-level alternatives.

As mentioned earlier, total student enrollment peaked in 1971 and then declined steadily until 1984, when the elementary-age group began to increase modestly. Expenditures for education in constant dollars bottomed out in the early 1980s but have been on the rise throughout the rest of the decade. The trend in average teacher salaries has nearly coincided with the enrollment trend, probably due, at least in part, to the aggregate decline in demand for teachers in the early to middle years of the 1980s. Since then, teacher salaries have shown an upward trend, although frequently not sufficient to offset the effects of inflation. U.S. Department of Education (1990) projections do not suggest significant increases in teacher salaries.

The U.S. Department of Education data and projections do not indicate any abatement in the need to recruit teachers. In fact, during the 1990s there will be a need for more teachers at the elementary and secondary school levels each year. The data in Table 2.8 show this projection for public schools. Clearly, the majority of the new hires will be to replace those who are leaving the classroom for a variety of reasons (retirement, other jobs, moving into administration or other roles). By the year 2000, using the moderate level of

Table 2.8. Demand for new classroom teachers in U.S. public elementary and secondary schools: 1989 to 2001 (in thousands).

Year	Total	For Enrollment Changes	For Turnover	For Other Factors
1989	185	20	141	24
1990	187	6	147	34
1991	200	35	152	13
1992	190	40	158	−8
1993	209	39	162	8
1994	208	39	168	1
1995	209	29	174	6
1996	217	26	177	14
1997	220	17	181	22
1998	218	7	187	24
1999	223	−7	192	38
2000	227	−10	197	40
2001	225	−14	199	40

Source: U.S. Department of Education, National Center for Education Statistics, 1990.

projection, the U.S. educational system must recruit annually almost 20,000 new teachers to meet the turnover or replacement requirements of the system.

If, as Tables 2.7 and 2.8 suggest, the need for teachers is a function of supply and demand, then the pool of potential teachers available for training and employment will be influenced by what teachers can command in salaries for their services. The data in Table 2.7 would indicate a system that is merely holding its own with regard to the actual purchasing power of teachers' salaries. The real expression of demand is the price, or salary, that an employer is willing to pay. Young people, who even now are making career decisions, are weighing all factors, including their earning power in the job market. The new teachers at the beginning of the 21st century will, by and large, be making their career choice in 1995 or 1996; and this decision will be influenced in part by the trends indicated in Tables 2.7 and 2.8. To have a positive impact on decisions to enter teaching in the 21st century, salaries and other benefits must be in place by the mid-1990s, or it will be too late to have the desired effect.

In looking at the impact of demographics on education, several issues can be identified. First, the size and location/concentration of minority populations, some of whom will not be English-speakers, will affect program planning in many school districts. Second, the burden of poverty falls disproportionately on minority groups. More than one-third of blacks were below the poverty level in 1989. Hispanics as a group also were generally less affluent than the non-Hispanic white population. For example, in 1988 the median family incomes were as follows:

U.S. Average:	$30,853
White Families:	$32,274
Hispanic Families:	$20,306
Black Families:	$18,098

The Asian population is a more diverse group in terms of economic status, with the Vietnamese being the least affluent segment of the Asian minority. The employment/unemployment data also reflect a similar disparity among ethnic groups.

The Educational Research Service (Bickers 1990) has reported that in 1988 one-third of the children born to women of the age group 18 to 44 years were in poor families with an annual income under $15,000. By 2000 a very large segment of the student population will be economically disadvantaged, placing a significant challenge

19

on the education system. The challenge becomes more complicated with the breakdown of the traditional American family. Hodgkinson (1991) points out that nearly half of the youth will spend at least some years before their 18th birthday in a single-parent household. Indeed, in the 1980s the "single female head" family increased by more than 35%, and the "single male head" family increased by more than 29%. The implications of family breakdown on students include problems in such areas as self-esteem, discipline, economics, and health.

In addition, a variety of social problems carry financial implications for schools. Examples include teenage pregnancy, drug use, and other problems related to at-risk youth. In responding to these problems, schools will need information, counseling, and support services, all of which will require additional financial resources. Failure to address these problems affecting youth likely will result in greater increases in the costs of welfare, mental health services, and law enforcement.

This cursory look at the demographics and trends provides a basis for some generalizations about the needs of America's schools as they enter the 21st century. By then, this nation will have a population of more than 260 million; and about 44 million pupils will be attending the nation's public elementary and secondary schools. Projections suggest the need for a major effort to recruit new teachers. This teaching force will be challenged to address the educational needs of ethnic minorities concentrated in major metropolitan areas. Further, these teachers must have the skills to cope with a wide variety of social and health issues that affect the learning of children and youth.

References

Bickers, Patrick M. *Demographic Influences on Education*. Arlington, Va.: Educational Research Service, 1990.

Frey, William H. "Are Two Americas Emerging?" *Population Today* (October 1991): 6-8.

Hodgkinson, Harold. "Reform versus Reality." *Phi Delta Kappan* 73 (September 1991): 8-16.

Hodgkinson, Harold. *California: The State and Its Educational System*. Washington, D.C.: Institute for Educational Leadership, 1986.

U.S. Bureau of the Census. *Statistical Abstract of the United States*. National Data Book, 111th edition. Washington, D.C.: U.S. Government Printing Office. 1991.

U.S. Bureau of the Census. *Projections of the Population of States, by Age, Sex, and Race: 1988 to 2010.* Current Population Reports, Series P-25, No. 1017. Washington, D.C.: U.S. Government Printing Office, 1989.

U.S. Bureau of the Census. *Projection of the Population of the United States by Age, Sex, and Race: 1988 to 2080.* Current Population Reports, Series P-25, No. 1018. Washington, D.C.: U.S. Government Printing Office, 1989.

U.S. Department of Education. *Projections of Education Statistics to 2001.* NCES Publication No. 91-683. Washington, D.C.: U.S. Government Printing Office, 1990.

U.S. Department of Education. *Digest of Educational Statistics: 1990.* NCES Publication 91-660. Washington, D.C.: U.S. Government Printing Office, 1991.

CHAPTER 3

School Finance Policy Goals, Criteria, and Outcomes

Since public education is an integral element in the economy of the nation and vital to the continuation of a democracy, it is an essential function of government. Thus states commit a major portion of their budgets to funding schools. But state funding systems for education did not develop in a vacuum. As state funding systems for schools have evolved in a philosophical, constitutional, and judicial context, goals for the school finance systems have been identified, criteria have been proposed, and outcomes have been specified. In this chapter, policy goals, criteria, and outcomes are explored followed by a discussion of the key elements required for an optimal state school finance system.

Public Policy Goals in School Finance

Local, state, and federal policymakers often must deal with a set of conflicting political and philosophical values when making decisions about policy goals for financing schools. In the last two decades, the traditional American values of equity, adequacy, and local choice have come into conflict.

America's system for financing schools was founded on the assumption that local government officials have the authority to choose the tax rate needed to operate their schools. Yet, in an effort to provide equity for both pupils and taxpayers, several court decisions since 1970 have challenged the concept of local school district choice in matters of school finance. Nevertheless, the value of local choice persists among the citizenry.

Several individuals have attempted to develop finance models that accommodate both equity and local choice (see Coons et al. 1970). However, efforts to reconcile these two values have been complicated by the additional dimension of ensuring adequacy in funding, so that all districts, regardless of their tax base, will have sufficient funding for schools without imposing an unreasonable burden on local taxpayers.

The Goal of Equity

The goal of equity is probably the most discussed but least understood. Even among school finance experts, there is not universal agreement on the meaning of equity. Essentially, equity in the context of school finance means equal treatment of persons in equal circumstances. From the pupil's perspective, equity means sufficient funding to ensure equal access to educational opportunity. From the taxpayer's perspective, equity means that taxes should be equal regardless of one's taxing jurisdiction. However, equity does not imply an adequate level of funding, only an equal level of funding for the pupil or an equal tax rate for the taxpayer. In the final analysis, equity is defined operationally by the public policy goal that guided the actions of the legislative body or by the decisions of the courts (Jordan and McKeown 1980). For example, a state school finance system could be equitable for pupils but not taxpayers, or vice versa.

Equity as applied to school finance can be horizontal or vertical. Horizontal equity assumes that all individuals are similar and should be treated in the same manner. However, individuals are not similar; they are different in many ways and have different needs. Thus the concept of horizontal equity is inadequate when applied to students in schools, because they have different educational needs.

The concept of vertical equity is more complex. It assumes that individuals are different and should be treated differently, because they have different needs. All pupils do not have the same educational needs. They have different abilities and capacities as well as different aspirations, all of which affect the level of funding required. In the same manner, taxpayers differ in their capacity to pay, and economic values vary for different parcels of property.

In their quest for vertical equity, state finance systems have recognized differences in educational needs by providing additional per-pupil funding for programs that cost more, such as services for the handicapped. This is commonly referred to as pupil weights. Almost half of the states allocate some of their funds on the basis of pupil weights (Salmon et al. 1988). An often quoted maxim to illustrate vertical equity is, "There is nothing so unequal as the equal treatment of unequals." The challenge facing school finance policymakers is to identify those differences that affect program costs and taxpayer capacity and to devise funding systems to accommodate those differences.

The Goal of Adequacy

The goal of adequacy is achieved when programs and learning opportunities are sufficient for a particular purpose. The determination of that purpose is a public policy decision. For example, with handicapped youth, adequacy might include the provision of an individualized educational program (I.E.P.), which is developed for each student in consultation with parents and a team of professional educators. For school finance purposes, the student's I.E.P. must be converted into those human services and materials needed for the desired program. Delivery of an adequate program does not assume equal per-pupil funding. In this case, the concept of vertical equity prevails, since unequal per-pupil funding is needed to provide an adequate program.

What is considered to be an adequate educational program, of course, will be influenced by a person's perspective on the circumstances of the situation. An employer's position on adequacy will be influenced by whether newly hired workers have the level of skills required to do a particular job in the firm. A superintendent's position on adequacy will be influenced by whether sufficient funds are available to carry out the educational program desired by the community. A school personnel director's position will be influenced by whether the salary schedule is competitive enough to attract and retain high quality faculty. A teacher's position is likely to be related to salary, working conditions, and support provided by the district. A principal's position on adequacy will be influenced by whether the budget provides the staff and materials/supplies required to operate the type of school sought by the community. A pupil's position will be influenced by whether the school provides learning experiences that are interesting and challenging. The parents' position will be influenced by how the school treats their children and whether their children are making satisfactory progress. Those interested in economic development will think that the schools are adequate when their perceived quality is sufficient to attract industry, and the tax burden is not so great as to drive industry away.

24

The Goal of Local Choice

The goal of local choice assumes that the local taxpayers and the school board should have the authority to establish the budget and set the tax levy for operating the schools. This tradition of local choice has resulted in a wide disparity in per-pupil expenditures among states and among districts within states. In low-wealth school districts with a limited tax base, local authorities can provide only the most basic educational program unless the state provides equalization assistance.

The traditional view on choice is quite different from the current emphasis on parental choice of the school that a child will attend. (Parental choice is discussed in the final chapter.) In the equity/choice dilemma, the privilege of unrestricted choice in per-pupil spending is in direct conflict with the goal of equity in per-pupil funding. Some proposals may intend to preserve the tradition of local choice; but, in fact, they present a false sense of choice. That is, with its limited tax base, the low-wealth school district has little power through choice to supplement a basic program unless the state provides equalization assistance.

Because of these unequal expenditures and unequal tax rates, several states have enacted legislation that imposes revenue or spending limitations. This has created a dilemma, with the goal of local choice in direct conflict with the goal of equity.

From this discussion of school finance goals, it is clear that systems for financing schools are imperfect and full of educational and political compromises. The goal of equity raises the most perplexing philosophical problem. While people can agree that current disparities in per-pupil expenditures are inequitable, they cannot agree at what point equity has been attained.

Criteria for Evaluating State School Finance Systems

State school finance systems vary considerably as they attempt to attain the goals of equity, adequacy, and local choice. These systems inevitably reflect a number of legislative compromises resulting from the need to spread limited resources over a variety of programs that benefit a range of constituents. State school finance systems can be analyzed and assessed using the following criteria: 1) stability and predictability, 2) responsiveness, 3) feasibility, 4) non-manipulability, and 5) ease of administration. Each of these criteria is discussed below.

Stability and Predictability

Stability and predictability are necessary in a state school finance system in order that planning may proceed in an orderly manner from one fiscal year to the next. However, because schools are financed through tax revenues, a change in the economic conditions can disrupt the stability of funding. For example, a decline in the assessed value of property or in state sales tax receipts will result in an immediate loss of revenues. For this reason, most experts contend that school funding should come from multiple tax sources, which respond in different ways to changing economic conditions. In this way, the criterion of stability and predictability is preserved.

Responsiveness

The criterion of responsiveness in a state school finance system is achieved if the system has the capacity to respond quickly to changes in economic and demographic conditions that affect district costs, such as general enrollment increases, increases in bilingual students, or increases in students with special needs who require a higher level of expenditure.

A balance between stability and responsiveness in the state school finance system is necessary to facilitate sound planning by local school districts. If local school districts face sudden enrollment increases, they want immediate recognition of this fact in the apportionment formula used by the state school finance system. On the other hand, if a district is facing declining enrollments, school officials are fearful of losing state funding because lowered enrollment does not immediately result in a reduction of educational budgets. In achieving the criterion of responsiveness, the finance system should be able to address changing conditions in ways that still provide adequate funding for all pupils and that reduce the disparities in per-pupil expenditures and in local tax rates.

Recently, some policymakers have advocated that school districts be funded on the basis of pupil performance. If such a reward/penalty factor were introduced into state school funding formulas, it would be difficult to maintain stability and responsiveness. If, for whatever reason, dramatic shifts in pupil performance occurred from one year to the next, districts would not have the stable funding needed for orderly operation. For example, low student performance could result in a loss of funds and force school districts to dismiss teachers, thus exacerbating the conditions that resulted in lowered pupil performance.

Feasibility

The criterion of feasibility is the extent to which the state school finance system is consistent with sound educational practices and existing economic realities. School finance systems should support maintenance of current programs as well as their continuing development and improvement. They should operate within the context of available revenues and competing demands for public funds. New and innovative programs can be funded as demonstration or pilot projects and then be institutionalized into the funding formula when they have demonstrated their effectiveness and are ready for general replication. The funding of any state school finance system should be subjected to a feasibility test in terms of the state's projected revenues and fiscal resources.

Non-Manipulability

The criterion of non-manipulability means that definitions and data used in state school funding formulas cannot be altered or modified so as to benefit a local school district. For example, districts might use local testing norms rather than state testing norms to increase the number of students eligible for remedial assistance. Student counts, program descriptions, and student admission requirements should be sufficiently precise so that local school officials cannot manipulate their data and reports to benefit their district unfairly.

Ease of Administration

The criterion of ease of administration means that the state finance system's requirements for reporting data do not impose an undue burden on local district personnel. As state school finance systems become more complex and expectations of schools increase, the requirements for data often increase. In deciding what data local school districts must submit to the state, it becomes important to differentiate between "nice to know" and "need to know." For example, should the state require that local districts submit data to develop a record file on each child in the state? Should the state require that the district maintain and submit financial records for each special program it operates? If so, how will these data be used?

Outcomes for a State School Finance System

While goals and criteria are essential elements of a state school finance system, the public increasingly is interested in the outcomes of the educational program. Put simply, the public wants to know what it is getting for the dollars it spends on education. Thus the public is asking school districts to demonstrate accountability, efficiency, and productivity.

Accountability

Accountability means that the local schools can demonstrate that they are operating in conformance with state statutes, using state funds as intended, and improving the performance of students in accordance with state goals. Few question the need for accountability; but many question how best to achieve it.

As more funds are expended for education, calls for accountability increase — usually in reference to pupil performance. But accountability needs to be examined in a broader context. The basic question is: Who is accountable to whom and for what? Rather than limiting accountability to pupil and teacher performance, it can be extended to parents, taxpayers, school board members, and legislators. Who is accountable for overcrowded classrooms with inadequate materials? Who is accountable for the fact that per-pupil expenditures and teacher salaries have not kept pace with inflation?

Efficiency

Efficiency means the prudent and optimum use of available funds in the day-to-day operation of schools. Concerns about efficiency often are expressed in calls for reducing administrative costs, increasing the use of educational technology, raising student performance, or cutting out the "frills" and returning to the basics.

State mandates designed to promote efficient operation of schools might be viewed as unnecessary meddling and interfering with local control of schools. Nevertheless, continued inefficient operation in a school district can result in state intrusion. One of the public policy challenges in financing public schools is how to maintain local control while preserving both state responsibility and local accountability.

Productivity

Productivity in the context of schools means the level of pupil performance as measured by some agreed-on standards. Measures of productivity might include scores on achievement tests, state and national awards, college admission rate, employment rate of graduates, and dropout rate, to name a few.

The effort to use the school finance system as a lever to increase educational productivity is a two-edged sword. Under decentralization and site-based decision making, one assumption is that school districts will have more autonomy to increase pupil performance or productivity; but with more autonomy comes greater accountability for the outcomes. A second assumption is that a program of incentives and recognition will contribute to increased productivity. Yet a finance system that is based on student productivity will find it difficult to address the criteria of stability and responsiveness. For example, if the state finance system is based on increased performance, then poorly performing students who need the greatest assistance will likely be penalized if the state reduces funding because students are achieving at a lower level.

Clearly, conflicts and contradictions are bound to arise in state school finance systems with regard to the goals, criteria, and outcomes discussed above. Not the least of the problems is confusion over the meaning of such goals as equity, adequacy, and choice. In the quest for equity and adequacy, some state finance formulas provide for uniform per-pupil spending. Other formulas, in the quest for taxpayer equity and local choice, permit variations in per-pupil spending but guarantee a foundation level of spending regardless of the local tax rate. Thus the level of funding is determined by the desires of local taxpayers and their elected officials. But as a result, pupil equity and adequacy may be sacrificed on the altar of local choice.

The first challenge facing policymakers responsible for the state school finance system is to balance the various goals while ensuring that all students have access to an adequately funded program suited to their needs. A second challenge is to provide equity for taxpayers so that tax rates and property assessments are equal across all school districts in the state. However, since tax rates and property assessments are matters of local control, it is difficult to see how true taxpayer equity is possible without giving up local control.

Further, the state's school finance system should provide each district with sufficient funds to provide all pupils with access to an adequate educational program appropriate to their individual needs. While the technical details of the funding system may vary, the ultimate goal should be to reduce the disparities among districts and move toward providing all students with an adequately funded educational program.

Optimal State School Finance System

The above discussion of goals, criteria, and outcomes reflects both the historical and the current situation regarding state school finance systems. The continuing quest for the optimal system has been frustrating and elusive because of the complexities involved in providing education for all students that is both equitable and adequate across all school districts in a state. With regard to the equity goal, there is the seemingly irresolvable issue as to whether equity can been achieved for both students and taxpayers. When the courts have entered the debate (see Chapter 5), their decisions have tended to indicate where funding is not equitable but have failed to define what equitable funding is.

Definitions of equity in state finance systems vary depending on the state's policy goal. For example, if the public policy goal is *student equity*, then the state's equalization formula provides equal per-pupil funding, while allowing for adjustments for special-needs students and other special conditions in school districts. But if the public policy goal is *taxpayer equity*, then equalization is attained by providing equal per-pupil funding based on equal levels of local tax effort, when adjustments have been made for the different educational needs of pupils and special conditions of districts.

These differing public policy goals are reflected in the two principal approaches to school finance. The first is the foundation formula, which is designed to provide equal per-pupil funding across the state. The dilemma with this approach is that the level of per-pupil funding may not be adequate or sufficient to ensure that all students have access to an educational program appropriate to their needs or aspirations. The second approach is the effort-oriented formula, which is designed to provide equal per-pupil funding for each locally determined unit of tax rate. The dilemma under this approach is that there can be wide variations in per-pupil funding among districts because of differences in the aspirations of decision makers in local school districts. (Types of state funding formulas will be discussed in the next chapter.)

Keeping in mind all the interacting factors that affect the funding of schools, the optimal state school finance system should contain at least the following components:

1. State-adopted goals for elementary and secondary schools; monitoring procedures to ensure that all the goals are addressed in each school district and individual school; and implementation of as-

sessment and reporting systems to provide policymakers and local citizens with evidence that all students are being served adequately and that progress is being made toward achievement of the state's educational goals.

2. Assurance that the goals of the state's school finance system are consistent with the state-adopted educational goals for elementary and secondary schools and that all pupils have equal access to an adequate educational program regardless of their place of residence. Further, there should be a clearly stated policy specifying a) whether the primary intent of the state school finance system is to provide equity for students and/or to taxpayers, b) whether local districts will have the right to choose their level of funding, and c) what evidence will be considered sufficient to demonstrate that the level of funding is adequate to ensure that all students have equal access to equivalent educational programs and services.

3. Recognition of the additional costs for serving special-needs students from preschool through grade 12 and assurances that such students will be provided with appropriate and adequately funded programs. Special-needs students should include, but not be limited to, the physically or psychologically impaired, the limited-English-speaking, the educationally and economically disadvantaged and those with other at-risk conditions, and the gifted and talented.

4. Recognition of the additional costs for certain school districts whose special conditions require additional funds in order to provide equivalent educational programs and services. Such special conditions in school districts should include, but not be limited to, sparsity or density of population, geographic isolation, cost of living, staffing differentials, and socioeconomic factors.

5. Recognition of the differences in the fiscal capacity of local districts to provide the physical facilities required to house the educational programs and meet state mandates. Such recognition should include, but not be limited to, state guarantees for local bonding power, state loan/grant programs, or equalization of local debt service obligations.

These components of an optimal state school finance program illustrate the range of concerns that confront legislators and others responsible for developing and implementing public policies related to funding schools.

References

Coons, J.E.; Clune, W.H., III; and Sugarman, S.D. *Private Wealth and Public Education*. Cambridge, Mass.: Belknap Press, Harvard University Press, 1970.

Jordan, K.F., and McKeown, M.P. "Equity in Financing Public Elementary and Secondary Schools." In *School Finance Policies and Practices*, edited by J.W. Guthrie. Cambridge, Mass.: Ballinger, 1980.

Salmon, R., et al. *State School Finance Programs 1986-87*. Blacksburg: American Education Finance Association, Virginia Polytechnic Institute and State University, 1988.

CHAPTER 4

State School Finance Equalization Systems

Until the early part of the 20th century, state funding for schools was meager and typically was allocated on a per-pupil basis. No adjustments were made for differences in taxable wealth among local school districts or for variations in educational requirements of students. Cubberley (1905) was an early advocate of the concept that states should equalize funds for local schools in order to assist low-wealth school districts. His early writings provided the impetus for the adoption of equalization as a basic concept in school finance. Out of this concept evolved a variety of state school finance equalization formulas during the period between Cubberley's early work in 1905 and Morrison's work in 1930.

The intent of these formulas is to operationalize the school finance goal of equity for students and taxpayers. Essentially, the formulas calculate a per-pupil entitlement from state and local revenues for each local school district, with a local district's funding calculated so that the state's payment is inversely related to the per-pupil wealth of the district. This is referred to as equalized funding. Through the formulas, the state demonstrates that it has a responsibility to provide a base level of funding for each pupil in the state. Through the equalization formulas, both pupils and taxpayers in all school districts are treated equally.

Local school officials hold different opinions about the efficacy of state equalization formulas. Although the formulas are designed so that the combination of state and local revenues results in an equal amount of funds per pupil, equalization assumes that a larger amount of state funds will go to school districts with lower taxable wealth per pupil. Local school officials in high-taxable-wealth districts often are critical of equalization because they receive proportionally less funding per pupil from the state than a district with low levels of taxable wealth. In fact, some high-taxable-wealth districts may

33

not receive any state funds because the yield of the required minimum tax rate exceeds their entitlement under the state equalization formula. Such districts are said to be "out of formula" or "budget-balanced."

Equalization in school funding does not necessarily result in equal amounts of per-pupil funding. Some state school finance systems are designed to accommodate variations in local tax rates or different aspiration levels of local districts. The amount per pupil supported from state and local funds may vary depending on the tax rate that the local officials choose to levy (Coons et al. 1970). Funding levels also may vary because the school finance system is designed to provide different levels of funding based on the educational requirements of special groups of students.

Types of State School Finance Systems

The impetus for state school finance systems began at the beginning of the 20th century with Cubberley's (1905) introduction of the flat grant. This approach did not solve the school finance problem because state funds were very limited and typically were distributed on a per-pupil basis irrespective of local wealth.

As state school finance systems evolved over the first few decades of this century, equalization models were developed to address the inequities occurring because of differences in taxable wealth among local school districts, with more state funds given to the less wealthy school districts. Over the years legislatures have modified the equalization models to accommodate their state's economic conditions and available resources. Therefore, the resulting state funding systems typically are not a pure representation of the original model developed in the 1920s. Among the states, the most frequently used approach is equalized foundation grants (Salmon et al. 1988).

At the time of the development and introduction of state school finance equalization models, urban districts were considered to be wealthy in that their principal source of local revenues was receipts from the property tax. In many respects, these early school finance systems were designed to benefit rural school districts in which both the quantity and quality of education were perceived to be low.

By the latter quarter of the 20th century, conditions in urban areas have changed dramatically. Urban areas now are perceived to have the most severe educational problems. Urban areas have a higher percentage of pupils needing expensive remedial programs; their stu-

34

dents are more mobile, often attending several schools in a single school year; costs of providing instruction are higher; and pressures to provide a broad range of social services are greater in inner-city areas. The first three conditions are referred to as "educational over-burden"; the fourth is called "municipal overburden."

School finance experts are in general agreement that finance formulas can and should be designed to compensate school districts for educational overburden, but there is less agreement on providing schools additional state funds to address the municipal overburden associated with providing a full range of municipal services (Jordan and Cambron-McCabe 1981). Some skeptics question whether addressing municipal overburden is justified when they review the range of services provided in some cities. Others acknowledge that there may be a need for assistance but that relieving the tax burden of municipalities should not be a function of the state school finance system.

Four funding models commonly used in state school finance systems are: flat grants, equalized foundation programs, local effort-oriented equalization programs, and full-state funding. Each of these models is discussed below.

Flat Grants

Flat grants were the earliest and most common system of state funding to local school districts. The system provided each district with an equal amount per student or teacher. Wealthy and poor school districts were treated equally. Later, legislators recognized that the poorer districts would need additional funds because of their low tax-paying ability. This led to the designation of special funds for the poor districts. Still later, the special funds were incorporated into equalization formulas, usually referred to as foundation programs. The following formula for allocating flat grants is similar in theory to full-state funding:

State Aid = (Number of Payment Units) × (Program Amount Per Unit)

To determine the district's entitlement, multiply the number of payment units (enrollment as determined by average daily attendance or average daily membership) by the allotted amount per unit. As shown in the following example, for 1,000 students and an allotted amount of $500 per pupil, the district would receive $500,000.

State Aid ($500,000) = 1,000 students × $500 per student

35

The original flat grant funds could be used for any legal educational purpose. Historically, North Carolina has used the flat grant as its primary funding system.

Even after the introduction of more complex equalization funding formulas, flat grants have continued to be used for allocating categorical funds for special-needs programs, such as special education and bilingual education. Flat grants also are used in some states to ensure that high-wealth school districts receive some state funds, even though they might not be eligible under the state's equalization formula. Such funding commonly is part of the political compromise negotiated by legislators from high-wealth districts, since their constituents typically are the source of a significant portion of the revenues in the state's general fund.

Foundation Programs

In the 1920s, George D. Strayer and Robert M. Haig (1923), both professors at Teachers College, Columbia University, built on the earlier original work of Cubberley and developed the Strayer-Haig fiscal equalization funding model, commonly referred to as the foundation plan.

This state/local cost-sharing plan has three basic steps. In the first step, the state determines the amount of funds per pupil or per teacher to be provided from the combination of state and local funds; this expression of educational need is designated the foundation amount. This amount may be adjusted to recognize the additional funds required for special-needs students. The second step is to determine the yield when the designated tax rate is applied to the assessed value of taxable property in the school district. The third step is to calculate the district's state aid by subtracting the district's local share in step two from the district's educational need in the first step. In most states using this plan, districts may supplement the foundation plan with additional local "leeway" funds; but the state usually does not provide additional state funds to equalize the local leeway revenues.

Educators are not in agreement concerning the merits of leeway or supplemental funding. Some contend that it is a desirable way to improve educational offerings and to retain some flexibility in the school funding system. Others contend that leeway funding results in inequities in per-pupil spending, because high-wealth districts can supplement funding with a very low tax rate whereas low-wealth districts cannot without excessive tax rates.

In their pure form, foundation formulas are easily understood and simple to calculate. However, they become more complicated as a result of legislators' efforts to accommodate different constituencies and to deal with special problems in the state. Some of the formula complications include incentives to start new programs, minimum payments per pupil, and hold-harmless provisions that result in high-wealth districts continuing to receive state funds even though they are not eligible for equalization payments. The basic foundation program is calculated using the following formula:

State Aid = [(Number of Payment Units) × (Program Amounts Per Unit)] − [(Local Tax Rate) × (Taxable Wealth)]

The first step in the calculation is to multiply the number of payment units times the state's payment per unit to determine the district's entitlement. For example, District A with 1,000 pupils or payment units and a program amount of $4,000 per unit would result in an entitlement of $4,000,000. If District A's local share were the yield from a tax rate of $1.00 per $100 of assessed property value times the $300,000,000 assessed value of taxable property, the local share would be $3,000,000, and the state's share would be $1,000,000. In another example, for District B with the same number of pupils but an assessed value of taxable property at $150,000,000, the local share would be $1,500,000 and the state payment would be $2,500,000. These examples illustrate the concept of equalization under which the state payments are greater to the less wealthy school district. The formulas for calculating state payments for Districts A and B are as follows:

District A
$1,000,000 (state aid) = [(1,000 × $4,000) = $4,000,000] − [(.001 × $300,000,000) = $3,000,000]

District B
$2,500,000 (state aid) = [(1,000 × $4,000) = $4,000,000] − [(.001 × $150,000,000) = $1,500,000]

One criticism of the foundation program is that the funding level per pupil or per teacher typically is only at the minimum level and is not sufficient to support an adequate educational program. A second criticism is that the foundation program has a stifling effect on funding for education, because the state does not provide funding beyond the minimum level.

Despite the criticisms, the foundation plan is the most prevalent system being used by states to fund public elementary and secondary schools. Currently, about two-thirds of the states use some modification of the equalized foundation program in allocating funds to local school districts (Salmon et al. 1988; Verstegen 1990).

Local Effort-Oriented Equalization Systems

About the same time that Strayer and Haig were developing the foundation concept, Harlan Updegraff (1922), a professor at the University of Pennsylvania, developed a local effort-oriented school funding approach. His school finance model was first referred to as "percentage equalization." Later variations of his basic model include "guaranteed tax base," "guaranteed tax yield," and "district power equalization."

Under these effort-oriented equalization formulas, local districts set the tax rate that determines the level of spending they wish to make. The state then provides the difference between the yield from that tax rate and a state guaranteed amount. With this state supplement, equal funding for every pupil is provided for both rich and poor school districts that tax at the same rate or spend the same amount per pupil. The basic principles of the local effort-oriented equalization programs are illustrated in the following formula for the guaranteed tax yield:

State Aid = [(State Guaranteed Dollars at Selected Tax Rate) × (Number of Payment Units)] − [(Selected Tax Rate) × (Taxable Wealth)]

To achieve equalization, state payments will be greater for less wealthy school districts and will vary according to the tax effort for districts of similar wealth. Unless the state places a ceiling on per-pupil spending or the tax rate, a local district could impose a higher tax rate to yield sufficient funds for the quality of program it wants. When this happens, school districts of similar wealth can have great variance in what they spend.

The first step in the calculation is to multiply the state guaranteed amount times the number of payment units to determine the district's entitlement. For example, if District A selected a tax rate of $1.25 per $100 of assessed value of taxable property with a total assessed value of $300,000,000 and the state guarantee was $40 per penny of tax rate, and the district had 1,000 pupils, the district's entitlement would be $5,000,000. District A's local share would be $3,750,000 from a tax rate of $1.25 per $100 of assessed value of property (expressed as 125 cents) times the $300,000,000 assessed value of property. The state payment would be the difference between the entitlement ($5,000,000) and the local share ($3,750,000), or $1,250,000. For District B with the same number of pupils and assessed value of property, but a tax rate of $1.00 per $100 (expressed as 100 cents), the local share would be $3,000,000 and the state payment would be $1,000,000. For District C with the same number of pupils and a similar tax rate of $1.00 per $100 (expressed as 100 cents) but an assessed value of $150,000,000, the local share would be $1,500,000 and the state payment would be $2,500,000. The calculation for Districts A, B, and C would be as follows:

District A

$1,250,000 (state aid) = [($40.00 × 125) × 1,000 = $5,000,000]
  − [(.0125 × $300,000,000) =
  $3,750,000]

District B

$1,000,000 (state aid) = [($40.00 × 100) × 1,000 = $4,000,000]
  − [(.0100 × $300,000,000) =
  $3,000,000]

District C

$2,500,000 (state aid) = [($40.00 × 100) × 1,000 = $4,000,000]
  − [(.0100 = $150,000,000) =
  $1,500,000]

These examples illustrate the concept of equalization under which the state payments are greater to the less wealthy school district, and the state payments will vary according to the tax effort for districts of similar wealth.

During the school finance reform movement in the late 1960s and early 1970s, the concept of "percentage equalization" was modified further and referred to as "district power equalization" (Coons et al. 1970). Under this system, local school districts could continue to set their level of funding; however, if the yield from the tax rate exceeded the state guaranteed amount, the excess would be captured and forwarded to the state treasury to use for less wealthy school districts.

In the late 1980s, seven states were using some modification of the local effort-oriented concept (Verstegen 1990). However, none of these states had a pure power equalization system with no limits on per-pupil spending or the local tax rate. In addition, no state was capturing all excess funds. In recent years, some states have moved to a two-tier financing system that includes a combination of a foundation plan and an equalized local-effort supplement. This combined method is being used in nine states (Verstegen 1990).

Full-State Funding

A few years after Strayer and Haig and Updegraff developed their approaches for state school finance systems, George Morrison (1930), professor at the University of Chicago, proposed a full-state funding model with all districts in the state operating as a single state district for financial purposes. This model was an attempt to deal with the inequity resulting from different levels of taxable property wealth among local school districts. Using this model, the state would be carrying out its responsibility of providing equal per-pupil expenditures regardless of where students lived. This model has the advantage of providing both pupil and taxpayer equity.

The distinctive element of the full-state funding model is that no local tax revenues are collected for support of the schools. Hawaii is the only state with full-state funding for public elementary and secondary schools. Prior to becoming a state, Hawaii's schools already were centralized under the territorial government. This centralized school system continued under statehood, as did the full-state system for funding schools.

Payment Units

Some unit measure is required for allocating state funds to local school districts on a fair and equitable basis. The principal methods used to determine this have been pupil or teacher units. Pupil units are based on the number of school-age persons in the district, the number of pupils officially enrolled in school, or the number of pupils actually attending school. Teacher units typically are based on a pupil-teacher ratio formula that provides a teacher for a specified number of students.

A frequently debated issue is whether the state school finance system should provide for students to be counted on the basis of average daily attendance (ADA) or average daily membership (ADM). In the first instance, students must be in attendance; in the second, students must only be on the roll.

40

Historically, ADA was the unit measure used to count students for state funding. ADA is computed by dividing the aggregate number of students in *attendance* during a specified period by the number of days in the period. This method benefits districts with high daily attendance and also encourages districts to take measures to keep absenteeism to a minimum. Thus ADA helps schools to enforce compulsory attendance statutes. Advocates for ADA emphasize that students must be in attendance to benefit from school.

Currently, ADM is more commonly used in state school finance formulas (Salmon et al. 1988). ADM is computed by dividing the aggregate number of students *enrolled* during a specified period by the number of days in the period. This method benefits districts with high absentee rates (often those having a high percentage of disadvantaged students) and districts with severe transportation problems. Advocates for ADM argue that the school must plan and staff on the basis of students on the rolls. Teachers, textbooks, and supplies must be available for each student whether or not that student is in attendance.

Pupil Units

Regardless of whether a state finance system uses ADA or ADM, the pupil unit has an advantage over the teacher unit as a basis for funding because it allows districts to vary class size for different instructional purposes.

As a refinement of the pupil unit, about half the states assign pupil weights or indices to account for different spending levels needed for different grade levels and other special and more expensive programs. Weights also may be used to recognize cost differences attributable to low student enrollment in the district. The use of pupil weights in state school finance systems was first advocated by Mort (1933).

The first use of pupil weights was to recognize the higher per-pupil expenditures needed to provide adequate instruction at different grade levels and in different subjects. A higher weight might be given to high school students because many of their classes have a limited number of work stations, such as in a science laboratory or in an advanced class with low enrollment. For example, if the state program per-pupil amount at 1.00 equals $4,000, a weight of 1.25 for a high school pupil would generate $5,000. Weights will be higher for students with special needs or disabilities because of small class size and the need for additional professional and support personnel.

41

In calculating pupil weights, teacher salaries are only one of the expenditure items. Salaries for teachers and services provided to the classroom by other personnel as well as instructional materials used by students are classified as "direct" expenditures. In addition, there are "indirect" expenditure items. These include the district's support and administrative services that serve the entire district, such as counselors, custodial and maintenance personnel, data processing, librarians, payroll, pupil transportation, purchasing, building principals, and the superintendent.

Pupil weights used in state school finance systems often are criticized because: 1) they usually are based on studies of "average practice" rather than "best practice" programs, 2) the amounts appropriated are not sufficient to pay the additional costs of programs in some districts, and 3) they require the labeling or categorizing of students in order to generate the funds. Arguments in support of using pupil weights are: 1) they allow districts more flexibility in organizing local programs to serve students, 2) differences among students and special conditions in some school districts can be accommodated without relying on fragmented categorical programs, and 3) the state can achieve an equitable funding system more easily. The challenges in using a pupil weight system are to isolate those programs whose cost differences can be justified on sound educational grounds, to devise weights that are appropriate to accommodate these differences, and to keep the weights current (Lyons and Jordan 1991).

Teacher Units

Allocation of funds based on teacher units typically uses a formula that provides one teacher for a specified number of students. The specified number might vary with grade level or type of class. For example, for a primary grade class, 20 pupils might be specified for a teacher unit; for a regular high school class, 25 pupils might be specified; and for a special education class, 10 pupils might be specified. At least five states use the teacher unit as the primary funding vehicle, and several more use teacher units for special programs.

Under both the pupil unit and teacher unit methods, the state school finance system can be used to encourage or discourage the introduction of special programs. For example, under the teacher unit method, controls can be put on the size of special education classes. Under the pupil unit method, separate state regulations could be used to control the size of classes.

42

Funding for Special Populations

Over the last three decades, states have established a variety of categorical programs to serve the educational needs of groups of students with special needs. Some of the original impetus for these programs came from the federal government in the form of competitive grants and demonstration programs. Some of the early federal initiatives were part of the "Great Society" programs of the 1960s; others were introduced after successful litigation guaranteeing an adequate education to bilingual students and children with disabilities. Thus it became generally accepted that it was in the national interest to provide federal and state funds to ensure that special populations have equal access to education.

These forms of differentiated funding are examples of vertical equity; that is, the funding systems recognize that providing adequate services for special-needs students is more costly than services for regular students. Thus vertical equity is achieved "when the quantity and mix of school resources and services vary in direct relationship to the discernible differences in the educational needs of students" (Chambers 1981, p.5).

States typically provide additional funding for the following programs: 1) special education, including the gifted and talented; 2) compensatory education; 3) bilingual education; 4) vocational education; and more recently 5) for at-risk youth. Depending on the availability of funds and the level of public support for specific programs, states use a variety of needs-based mechanisms to allocate funds to local school districts for these programs.

One of the continuing policy questions is whether state funds for special populations should be included in the general state-aid formulas, which are subject to equalization calculations, or whether there should be separate categorical funding. Advocates for separate funding for special populations argue that if funding is earmarked, it will more likely be used for the client groups for whom it is intended. Further, they contend that increases in funding for special groups are more likely if funding is separate. The opposite position is that securing adequate funding for all students will be enhanced if programs and services are funded through the general state-aid system.

Needs-Based Funding Mechanisms

A variety of mechanisms are used in allocating funds for programs and services for special students. Among the most widely used are:

43

pupil weights, categorical grants, competitive discretionary grants, excess and percentage cost reimbursements, unit cost adjustments, and index of need. Each of these is discussed briefly in the following paragraphs.

Pupil weights. Under pupil weights, the state establishes different per-pupil indices in order to provide programs and services that are more costly than the average per-pupil costs (Webb et al. 1988). Typically, a weight of 1.00 is assigned to students in intermediate grades who are not in special programs; different weights are assigned to other students based on the comparative expenditures for their grade level or specialized program.

Categorical funding. An alternative to pupil weights is to use separate categorical grants for allocating state monies for special populations. These categorical grants are in addition to the basic per-pupil allocations and are based on the number of eligible students, classrooms, or teachers in a special program. The grants may be a fixed amount per student or a percentage of the approved cost for educating a particular group of students. Typically, categorical grants are not subjected to equalization calculations; that is, all school districts receive the same amount per student or teacher irrespective of the local district's taxable wealth.

Competitive discretionary grants. When state funds are limited and not sufficient to justify funding special programs in all school districts, or if states and the federal government want to encourage pilot demonstration/research projects, they often establish competitive grant programs. Under these programs, school districts must compete for limited funds by submitting a proposal in which the district agrees to comply with the applicable state or federal laws and regulations. The program proposal is reviewed on its merits, and awards are made to the school districts whose applications best meet the criteria established by the funding agency (Sherman 1987).

Excess cost reimbursement. Some states use the excess cost mechanism to fund local district programs for students with special needs. The excess cost is the difference between the cost of educating a regular student and that of a student enrolled in a special program. The state may pay all of the excess cost or a percentage of the amount. Formulas for excess cost reimbursement require detailed cost-accounting procedures, because the reimbursement is based on actual expenditures (Hartman 1980).

Unit cost adjustment. This mechanism is used to fund a district's entitlement based on the number of teachers or classroom units needed for special programs rather than on the actual number of students in the program (Webb et al. 1988). State standards usually prescribe minimum and maximum class sizes in order for a school district to receive state funding for a classroom or a teacher (Hartman 1980).

Index of need. This funding mechanism is a recent development in needs-based funding. With the index of need method, pupil counts or pupil weights are not used in calculating the amount of funding. Rather, the index is a proxy for the magnitude of need in a given school district. Quantifiable indicators are selected to provide a composite view of the relative magnitude of need. As an example, for a compensatory education program, the indicators used in calculating the index of need for a district or school might include the number of children from low-income families, number of students scoring below the 40th percentile on standardized achievement tests, and number of students who have been in their school for two years or less.

Since this funding mechanism is still in its developmental stages, several issues relative to its use have yet to be resolved. The two major issues are the relative importance of individual indicators when multiple indicators are used and the collection of valid and reliable data that cannot be manipulated by local districts to increase their state allocation.

Funding for Special Education

The impetus for state and federal funding for special education programs to serve handicapped or disabled youth came from a series of court cases in the 1970s. This litigation and a general social concern led to the enactment of P.L. 94-142, the Education of All Handicapped Children Act, in 1975 and its subsequent amendment, Individuals with Disabilities Education Act (IDEA), in 1990. As a result of this legislation, states have had to develop programmatic funding for special education.

The purpose of these federal programs is to help school districts provide programs and services to persons with disabilities between the ages of 3 and 21. In the 1990-91 school year, approximately 4.4 million special education students were being served in elementary and secondary schools. Even though the federal requirements for programs and services are quite prescriptive, federal funding ($1.5 billion) represents about 4% percent of the total costs of serving these students (NEA 1991). The responsibility for most of the funding rests with the states and local school districts.

State funding mechanisms for special education fall into six broad categories: 1) pupil weights, 2) instructional units, 3) formulas for percentage reimbursement for excess cost of programs, 4) flat grants, 5) full-state funding, and 6) combination methods (Verstegen and Cox 1990). In 1987-88, 18 states used some form of pupil weights, 8 states used the instructional unit method, 15 states used excess cost or percentage reimbursement, and 10 states used either flat grants, full-state funding, or a combination of methods.

State funding levels for special education often are inadequate to ensure that each child is provided with a free and appropriate education. The amounts provided through the pupil weights or unit cost reimbursements often are insufficient because the program cost data have not been updated to reflect current expenditures, the base support level is inadequate, or cost variations among districts are so great that use of the same formula for all districts is unrealistic. Given these conditions, unless a state uses the excess cost reimbursement mechanism, a disproportionate share of the cost of special education may well fall on the local school district.

Funding for Compensatory Education

The principal source of funding compensatory education for the educationally disadvantaged is the federal government. Funds are allocated through Chapter 1 of the Education Consolidation and Improvement Act of 1981, using a formula that includes the number of students from low-income families and the average per-pupil expenditure in the state. The largest portion of the program funds is distributed to local school districts through the basic grant program ($4.4 billion in 1990). The remaining funds are used to support three state-administered programs for handicapped youth, migrant youth, and neglected and delinquent youth (Irwin 1991). Virtually all school districts receive some Chapter 1 funds. In 1990-91 the funding level for school districts was sufficient to serve about 5.5 million students, or about 65% of the total number of eligible students (NEA 1991).

Federal funds for education of the disadvantaged have not kept pace with the continuing rise in educational costs and the increasing number of eligible disadvantaged youth. Since federal funding has been inadequate to serve all educationally disadvantaged youth, several states have shared in the funding of these programs. As of 1990, 32 states were providing state funds to local school districts to conduct compensatory education programs. The states' share of the total cost of local programs ranged from 7% to 56% (Irwin 1991).

Given the projected increases in the number of children living in poverty and disadvantaged environments, the need for compensatory programs will become ever more important. The need will be particularly critical in states with increasing low-income and minority populations. A recent study in Texas (Reyes 1991) suggests that state and federal allocations to local districts are not sufficient to fund the educational needs of an increasing number of students qualifying for compensatory education services. To provide the programs and services these students need, districts will have to divert funds from their regular, mainstream programs. Compounding this problem are the increasing demands for accountability as measured by student achievement. Districts will have difficulty achieving substantial increases in student achievement without addressing the educational needs of the lowest quartile of the student body, which, for the most part, consists of those students who are eligible for compensatory education programs.

Funding for Bilingual Education

With the current influx of immigrants from Eastern Europe, Southeast Asia, the Caribbean, and Latin America, schools are faced with the need to provide special programs for increasing numbers of students with no or limited English proficiency. Some urban schools have as many as 20 different native languages represented in the student body. These students will need to become proficient in English if they are to succeed in school. This will require extra funding for special staff and materials.

One of the continuing debates is over what kind of program is most appropriate for students with no or limited proficiency in English. Some advocate the English-as-a-second-language approach. Others prefer bilingual programs in which initial instruction is in the student's native language with a gradual transition to instruction in English. Still others argue for English immersion classes in which students develop fluency in English as quickly as possible so that they can be placed in regular classes. Another issue in bilingual education is how much responsibility the school has for helping students develop a better understanding of and appreciation for their native culture.

Federal funds for bilingual education are provided through the Bilingual Education Act, which provides discretionary grants to school districts for students whose native language is other than English and who have difficulty in reading, writing, and understanding English

47

(Irwin 1991). In the 1990-91 school year, about 250,000 students with limited English proficiency were served by the federal bilingual education programs. Approximately 50% of the federal funds for elementary and secondary education bilingual programs were allocated to three states: California, New York, and Texas. However, federal funds have never been sufficient to assist all students needing bilingual education programs. In fact, in the last decade, federal funds for bilingual education, when adjusted for inflation, have decreased about 47% (NEA 1991).

When faced with a lack of federal funds, school districts have had to allocate more funds from their regular budget to maintain their bilingual education programs. The problem is exacerbated in some schools with marked increases in the number of students with limited English proficiency.

Recent surveys indicate that 25 states provide specific funds for bilingual education (Verstegen 1990). Funding patterns vary among the states. In 12 states, funds are included in the basic school support program with allocations made through pupil weights or instructional units. In two states, the state pays the excess cost for the bilingual program over the cost of the regular education program. Categorical grant allocations are used in eight states. Hawaii provides full-state funding; California funds bilingual education through the state compensatory education program; and West Virginia provides only state-level funding.

Funding for Vocational Education

Interest in vocational and technical education programs has increased as national attention has focused on developing a more competitive workforce. As technologies increase in sophistication, the schools must be able to provide classrooms with state-of-the-art equipment and develop new instructional approaches appropriate for a technological society. Many school districts are developing school/business partnerships and cooperative work programs in an effort to infuse private-sector technological expertise into their voc-tech programs as well as to maximize their limited fiscal resources.

The original impetus for federal funding of vocational education programs was the Smith-Hughes Act of 1917, which continues to support local programs to this day. More recent federal legislation is the Carl D. Perkins Vocational and Applied Technology Act, which provides grants to states to "improve education programs that en-

hance economic and vocational competencies required by a techno-
logically advanced society" (Irwin 1991). Most of the Perkins Act
funds are allocated by formula to the states. Each state is required
to submit a plan for administering vocational and technical education programs operated by local school districts, a consortium of districts, or post-secondary education institutions.

A 1984 study indicated that the federal share of total expenditures
for vocational education was about 8%. However, the 1991 funding
level represented a decrease of 29% since 1980, when adjusted for
inflation (Irwin 1991). The U.S. Department of Education is developing a new system for tracking vocational education students to determine total expenditures.

Funding Programs for At-Risk Youth

A decade ago public policy discussions on education had little to
say about the problems of youth at risk of not completing high school.
The prevailing attitude was that a significant number of youth would
leave school but could still get low-skill jobs in the labor market.
This attitude of benign neglect began to change as a result of disruption of the American family structure, employment shifts in the job
market, and social problems related to teenage pregnancy and drug
and alcohol abuse. Moreover, national concern began to be expressed
about the declining performance of American students in general and
the need to become more competitive in the world economy.

Today, the interest in improving educational opportunities for at-
risk youth is high. This interest has been reinforced recently by the
National Education Goals adopted by President Bush and the nation's
governors (National Governors' Association 1990). Some of these
goals are targeted directly at the at-risk youth population.

Both economists and educators state that it is critical for these students to be adequately educated for the future well-being and economic growth of the nation (Committee for Economic Development
1987; Levin 1989). Levin argues for funding programs for at-risk
youth because of the cost to society if these youth are neglected. He
states that the costs to society include: 1) the creation of a dual-class
society, 2) disruption of higher education, 3) reduced national and
state economic competitiveness, and 4) higher public service costs
associated with poverty and crime. For these reasons, Levin asserts
that "the social benefits of such investments are likely to be well in
excess of the costs" (Levin 1989, p. 52).

Levin goes on to hypothesize that a serious effort to cope with this problem would require an additional appropriation in excess of $25 billion annually. Compare this with the estimated annual cost of the current dropout problem of $71 billion in lost tax revenue, $3 billion in increased expenditures related to welfare and unemployment, and $3 billion in crime-related costs (see Grossnickle 1986; Hodgkinson 1986; Kunisawa 1988; and Natriello, Pallas, and McDill 1987). Such high social and economic costs suggest that preventive actions in the form of programs for at-risk youth would be a cost-effective investment.

During the past several years, state policymakers have responded to the problem by allocating funds targeted at dropout prevention and for programs to serve at-risk youth. Several state efforts, particularly those in California, Florida, New York, and North Carolina, have been funded at relatively high levels (Sherman 1987). These efforts were confirmed in a national survey dealing with definitions of at-risk youth and state funding practices (McDonough 1990).

One of the problems in developing and funding programs for at-risk youth is that a precise and uniformly accepted definition for at-risk youth does not exist. McDonough (1990) found that 29 states had no official definition of at-risk youth. In 13 states, definitions were limited to academic performance. Definitions in eight states included both academic performance and socioeconomic characteristics.

Specific funding was not being provided in 33 states, but 21 of those states did provide funds targeted at segments of the at-risk population, such as pregnant teenagers. These funds were distributed primarily through competitive or categorical grants. Specific funding was being provided for at-risk programs in 17 states. In these states, funds were being allocated through competitive grants in eight states, through formula-based mechanisms in six states, and through a combination of competitive grants and formulas in three states.

Approaches for funding state programs to serve at-risk youth have evolved in a different manner from the needs-based funding approaches used for special education programs. School districts seeking to serve at-risk youth have come up with a variety of program approaches reflecting local priorities and needs. Many of these programs are highly innovative and, in some cases, have resulted in the restructuring of the total educational setting in order to better meet the needs of all students.

Programming for at-risk youth is still evolving, and there appears to be strong support for encouraging local school district creativity, diversity, and flexibility in designing and delivering programs. One concern is the absence of extensive program evaluation data and cost-effectiveness studies; however, the consensus appears to be that immediate action is justified because the social and economic costs are too great to delay action.

Lyons (1990), in a cost and evaluation study of funding mechanisms for at-risk programs, identified the following policies for states to consider when selecting funding mechanisms that would maximize local innovation and decision making:

1. Immediate attention should be given to funding programs and services for at-risk youth because the social and economic cost of ignoring these youth is too great.

2. Variations in per-pupil costs for the delivery of similar programs are so great that funding on the basis of a uniform per-pupil allocation statewide would be premature. More information is needed on program effectiveness and the comparative costs in different settings.

3. Funding based on an equalization formula would tend to penalize large urban school districts with a high proportion of at-risk youth and high taxable wealth. Thus the local fiscal burden to provide the program would be disproportionate.

4. The index of need is the most efficient funding mechanism to use if the intent is to foster local program flexibility, to avoid labeling of students, and to target funds for the districts with the highest incidence of at-risk youth. The challenge in using the index as a funding mechanism is to identify those variables that are most appropriate for the circumstances in a given state.

As states gather more data on program effectiveness and costs, they will be in a better position to establish priorities for programs for special-needs students. With increased attention given to accountability and student outcomes, state policymakers may begin to use funding mechanisms to encourage program innovations and other promising changes in local districts.

References

Brodinsky, B. *Students at Risk: Problems and Solutions*. AASA Critical Issues Report. Arlington, Va.: American Association of School Administrators, 1989.

Chambers, J.G. "Cost and Price Level Adjustments to State Aid for Education: A Theoretical and Empirical Review on Educational Need and Fiscal Capacity." In the 2nd Annual Yearbook of the American Education Finance Association, *Perspectives in State School Support Programs*, edited by K.F. Jordan and N. Cambron-McCabe. Cambridge, Mass.: Ballinger, 1981.

Committee for Economic Development. *Children in Need: Investment Strategies for the Educationally Disadvantaged*. New York, 1987.

Coons, J.E.; Clune, W.H., III; and Sugarman, S.D. *Private Wealth and Public Education*. Cambridge, Mass.: Belknap Press, Harvard University Press, 1970.

Cubberley, E.P. *School Funds and Their Apportionment*. New York: Teachers College, Columbia University, 1905.

Davis, W.E., and McCaul, E.J. *At-Risk Children and Youth: A Crisis in Our Schools and Society*. Orono: University of Maine, 1990.

Fine, M. "Why Adolescents Drop Into and Out of Public High School." In *School Dropouts: Patterns and Policies*, 2nd ed., edited by G. Natriello. New York: Teachers College Press, 1987.

Grossnickle, D.R. *High School Dropouts: Causes, Consequences, and Cure*. Fastback 242. Bloomington, Ind.: Phi Delta Kappa Educational Foundation, 1986.

Hahn, A.; Danzberger, J.; and Lefkowitz, B. *Dropouts in America: Enough Is Known for Action: A Report for Policymakers and Grantsmakers*. Washington, D.C.: Institute for Educational Leadership, 1987.

Hartman, W.T. "Policy Effects of Special Education Funding Formulas." *Journal of Education Finance* (Fall 1980): 135-59.

Hodgkinson, H. *California: The State and Its Educational System*. Washington, D.C.: Institute for Educational Leadership, 1986.

Irwin, P.M. *U.S. Department of Education: Major Program Trends, Fiscal Years 1980-1991*. CRS Report to Congress 91-10 EPW. Washington, D.C.: Congressional Research Service, Library of Congress, 1991.

Jordan, K.F., and Cambron-McCabe, N.H., eds. *Perspectives in State School Support Programs*. Cambridge, Mass.: Ballinger, 1981.

Kunisawa, B.N. *A Nation in Crisis: The Dropout Dilemma*. Washington, D.C.: National Education Association, 1988.

Levin, H.M. "Financing the Education of At-Risk Students." *Education Evaluation and Policy Analysis* (Spring 1989): 47-60.

Lyons, T.S. "Alternative State Funding Allocation Methods for Local School District Programs to Serve 'At-Risk' Youth." Doctoral dissertation, Arizona State University, 1990.

Lyons, T.S., and Jordan, K.F. "Development of Expenditure Indices for Programs to Serve At-Risk Youth." *Journal of Education Finance* 16, no. 4 (1991): 431-45.

Mann, D. "Can We Help Dropouts: Thinking About the Undoable." In *School Dropouts: Patterns and Policies*, 2nd ed., edited by G. Natriello. New York: Teachers College Press, 1987.

McDonough, J.T. "A Survey of Opinions and Attitudes Toward State 'At-Risk' Program Focus, Delivery, and Funding." Doctoral dissertation, Arizona State University, 1990.

Morrison, H.C. *School Revenue*. Chicago: University of Chicago Press, 1930.

Morrison Institute for Public Policy. *1988-89 Status and Evaluation Report: The Arizona At-Risk Pilot Project: Serving Students in Grades K-3 and 7-12 Pursuant to HB 2217*. Tempe: School of Public Affairs, Arizona State University, November 1989.

Mort, P.R. *State Support for Public Education*. Washington, D.C.: American Council on Education, 1933.

National Education Association (NEA). *The Cost of Excellence*. Washington, D.C., July 1991.

National Governors' Association. *National Education Goals*. Washington, D.C., 1990.

Natriello, G.; Pallas, A.M.; and McDill, E.L. "Taking Stock: Renewing Our Research Agenda on Causes and Consequences of Dropping Out." In *School Dropouts: Patterns and Policies*, 2nd ed., edited by G. Natriello. New York: Teachers College Press, 1987.

Orr, M.T. *Keeping Students in School*. San Francisco: Jossey-Bass, 1987.

Ralph, J. "Improving Education for the Disadvantaged: Do We Know Whom to Help?" *Phi Delta Kappan* 70 (January 1989), 395-401.

Reyes, A. "The Cost of Educating Secondary Compensatory Education Students." *IDRA Newsletter* 18 (November 1991).

Salmon, R., et al. *State School Finance Programs 1986-87*. Blacksburg: American Education Finance Association, Virginia Polytechnic Institute and State University, 1988.

Sherman, J.D. *Strategies for Financing State Drop-Out Programs*. Washington, D.C.: Pelavin Associates, 1987.

Strayer, G.D., and Haig, R.M. *The Financing of Education in the State of New York*. Report of the Educational Finance Commission 1. New York: Macmillan, 1923.

Updegraff, H. *Rural School Survey in New York State: Financial Support*. Ithica, N.Y., 1922.

Verstegen, D.A. *School Finance at a Glance*. Denver: Education Commission of the States, April 1990.

Verstegen, D.A., and Cox, C.L. *State Models for Financing Special Education*. Charlottesville: Department of Educational Leadership and Policy Studies, Curry Memorial School of Education, University of Virginia, 1990.

Webb, L.D.; McCarthy, M.; and Thomas, S. *Financing Elementary and Secondary Education*. Columbus, Ohio: Merrill, 1988.

Wehlage, G.G., and Rutter, R.A. "Dropping Out: How Do Schools Contribute to the Problem?" *Teachers College Record* 87, no. 3 (1986).

CHAPTER 5

The Courts and School Finance*

Since 1970 state programs for financing the public schools have faced court challenges in about 35 states (LaMorte 1989). Litigation has been initiated in both federal and state courts; however, the principal arena has been in the state courts. Following the rejection of the plaintiffs' pleas by the U.S. Supreme Court in *San Antonio* v. *Rodriguez* (1973), some observers thought that the role of the judiciary would diminish, but that has not happened. The sustained litigation challenging state school finance programs focuses on the technical provisions of the state constitutions rather than provisions in the federal Constitution.

Each state constitution contains provisions for education; these provisions and others related to due process and taxation typically serve as the basis for litigation challenging the existing system's inequity for both for students and taxpayers. In contrast to the school desegregation decisions, the courts typically have not imposed a remedy but only indicated what needs to be fixed. The "fixing" thus becomes the responsibility of the legislative process. However, few are satisfied with the solutions; and litigation continues, for example, in California, New Jersey, and Texas.

Typically, the point in contention is that the existing state school funding system results in wide disparities in per-pupil expenditures among local school districts creating unequal educational opportunity. As discussed later in greater depth, the courts have established the legal principle that since education is a responsibility of state government, the state has an obligation to provide each child in the state with equal access to an educational program.

The basic research for and initial draft of this chapter was prepared by Mark Ebert, staff attorney, University of Arizona.

The key issue in the litigation is the effect of a state school finance system that uses local property tax as a major source of revenue for schools. Since there is a wide disparity in the taxable wealth per pupil among local school districts, the tax rate to provide an equivalent level of per-pupil funding among districts would have to vary considerably. This condition is perceived to be unfair to both taxpayers and students.

Of the decisions issued by state supreme courts so far, 10 have upheld the existing provisions of the state school finance system, and eight have held the system to be unconstitutional. In the decisions that have upheld the existing funding systems, the courts have acknowledged education to be an important function of the state but not a fundamental right under which the state guarantees equal treatment for all students. In some instances, the courts have been critical of the financing systems but have indicated that the problem should be resolved by legislative action rather than by judicial decisions.

In the decisions that have invalidated school finance programs, the courts have held that the current system was unconstitutional on the grounds of unfairness to both taxpayers and students. Unequal tax burdens on taxpayers were considered to be in violation of the equal protection provisions of the state constitutions. Disparities in per-pupil expenditures were deemed to be in violation of equal protection provisions of the state constitutions or the technical provisions of the state constitution pertaining to education (LaMorte 1989).

One of the most significant decisions came from the Kentucky State Supreme Court in *Rose* v. *Council for Better Education* (1989). In this case the state's entire elementary and secondary education system was found to be in violation of the state constitution. The state legislature had to enact legislation that met the standards set by the court by a specific date or the entire state system of education would have been dissolved. The ruling covered the organization of local school districts, the state board of education, and the state department of education, as well as the state financing system.

The decision in Kentucky was in striking contrast to the traditional way in which decisions are made about school funding. Traditionally, interest groups representing parents, corporate taxpayers, and advocates for other public services seek to influence the funding process by lobbying legislators or persuading voters to approve or reject referenda for schools. Because these processes have resulted in many inequities, advocates for fairness in school funding have sought relief through the courts in the belief that the courts are more insulated from political influence. As a result, the courts in Kentucky and other states have been an avenue for changing public school finance policy.

The involvement of the courts in education funding mechanisms is not new; it began in the 1800s with an early Kansas decision (*State v. Freeman*) that required the county commissioners to raise the funds to establish a high school. Since this early decision, the position of the courts has followed several distinct trends. The following discussion focuses on the constitutional bases involved in school funding litigation and analyzes the courts' holdings that have established the constitutional parameters on public school finance.

Constitutional Analysis

In the United States, public education is the responsibility of state governments. Education is not specifically mentioned in any of the articles of the U.S. Constitution, which enumerate the powers of the three branches of the federal government. Thus control over public education remains with the states. This tradition dates from Colonial times. Federal legislation affecting education is justified under the general welfare clause in the Preamble to the U.S. Constitution.

States exercise control over public education through the provisions of their state constitutions and by state legislative actions. These provisions have led to the establishment of state education departments, chief state school officers, and local school districts. The school districts are arms of the state and are considered political subdivisions. They receive state funding through such sources as legislative appropriations, tax revenue derived from the collection of levies on real property located within the district, and monies collected from the sale of bonds. With education being a function of the state, provisions for funding schools are viewed as "state actions" and, therefore, must be conducted in a manner consistent with the individual state constitutions and those provisions of the U.S. Constitution that place constraints on the activities of government.

Because education is not mentioned in the U.S. Constitution, litigants in school finance cases typically base their constitutional claims on the equal protection clause, which says that "No State shall . . . deny to any person within its jurisdiction the equal protection of the laws." Parallel claims also are often made if the state constitution contains an equal protection clause. The basic premise is that a funding mechanism is unfair or fiscally irresponsible if it results in different schools receiving different amounts of funds. Plaintiffs claim that the state, through its school finance system, is failing to provide equal protection for its students because of the different levels of funding. Once it has been determined that the state has taken action to fund the schools, equal protection analysis involves the judicial application of differing standards of review to the finance laws.

The applicable standard depends on how the laws classify individuals into groups and how members of the groups are treated differently. Because any statute is bound to treat some people differently from others, the equal protection question is: What is the basis for the differential treatment? Generally, the different treatment must bear a sufficient relationship to a legitimate governmental purpose for the laws to survive a constitutional challenge. The principal applicable standards are discussed in the following paragraphs.

Strict Scrutiny

The highest standard of review is referred to as "strict scrutiny." The U.S. Supreme Court first established standards of review for equal protection claims in *Korematsu* v. *United States* (1944), which dealt with internment of persons of Japanese descent living in the United States during World War II. *Korematsu* was the first case to apply strict scrutiny. At issue in the case was the unfavored treatment by the government of persons of Japanese descent for the purpose of promoting national security in time of war. The Court held that when a classification is based on a characteristic such as national origin, the classification will be "suspect." Therefore, the government must demonstrate that the classification is narrowly tailored to promote a compelling interest. If the classification is not narrowly tailored or not the least restrictive means available to achieve the desired end, it violates the equal protection guarantee.

In *Korematsu*, the challenged action survived the strict scrutiny test, because the Court believed the internment was justified by the military's apprehension of the imminent danger of an invasion of the West Coast. Thus race and national origin became "suspect classes." The Supreme Court has declined to find that any other type of classification is suspect, and it has never again found a governmental purpose compelling enough or a means narrowly drawn enough to survive a strict scrutiny test (Nowak and Rotunda 1991).

In addition to suspect class situations, the strict scrutiny standard of review also will be applied by the court when the nature of the treatment involves the restriction of a fundamental right. Fundamental rights are those explicit freedoms enumerated in the first 10 Amendments to the U.S. Constitution and those rights that the U.S. Supreme Court has determined to be implicit. Once again, the restriction will be permissible only if a compelling governmental interest is involved and the restriction is narrowly tailored to achieve that interest. The six implicit fundamental rights and freedoms that trigger a strict scrutiny review are: 1) freedom of association, 2) freedom of participation in the electoral process (*Reynolds* v. *Sims* 1964), 3) freedom of travel (*Shapiro* v. *Thompson* 1969), 4) freedom to a fair process to resolve individual claims against the government, 5) right to fairness in the criminal law process, and 6) right to privacy (*Griswold* v. *Connecticut* 1965).

Rational Basis

The lowest standard of review is referred to as "rational basis." Under this level of review are classifications relating to economics or general social welfare. For example, this test surfaces in cases examining discrimination on the basis of wealth and age, since neither of these conditions has been considered to be either a suspect class or a fundamental right. The rational basis test requires that the classification rationally relate to a legitimate governmental purpose. The U.S. Supreme Court has applied a rational basis test when examining methods used by government to allocate governmental subsistence payments (*Dandridge* v. *Williams* 1970), housing (*Arlington Heights* v. *Metropolitan Housing Development Corp.* 1977), and government employment (*Massachusetts Board of Retirement* v. *Murgia* 1976, and *Harrah Independent School District* v. *Martin* 1979).

Substantial Relationship

Finally, the U.S. Supreme Court has articulated an intermediate standard of review called "substantial relationship." The test at this level requires the presence of a substantial relationship to an important governmental interest. Classifications reviewed under this standard include gender (*Craig* v. *Boren* 1976) and illegitimacy (*Reed* v. *Campbell* 1986). However, individual justices often make their own evaluations of the asserted governmental interest, making the meaning of this test less than clear (Nowak and Rotunda 1991, p. 743).

The test to be applied when reviewing the constitutionality of public education funding was decided directly in *San Antonio Independent School District* v. *Rodriguez*. Here the plaintiffs challenged the public school financing system used in Texas. In deciding this landmark case, the U.S. Supreme Court held that access to a public education is not a fundamental right under the U.S. Constitution. The Court indicated that the rational basis test was the appropriate standard when using the U.S. Constitution to review laws relating to public education. Therefore, under the federal equal protection clause, a state school funding system need only pass the rational basis test. If the government can demonstrate that the classification promotes a legitimate purpose, the funding scheme will be upheld under the precedent set by *Rodriguez*.

Under the principles of constitutional law, both federal courts and state courts have the authority to interpret federal law, but the final decision rests with the U.S. Supreme Court (Wright 1983). State courts have the authority to interpret their own state constitutions, but the final decision rests with the highest court in the state. As a result of the *Rodriguez* decision, advocates of school finance reform have turned to state courts and state constitutions in their efforts to challenge the constitutionality of public school finance systems. So long as the application of a state constitutional provision does not restrict or conflict with protections afforded by the federal constitution or intrude on an area pre-empted by the federal government (for example, national defense), states are free to use their own constitutions to achieve results not available under the federal constitution.

Early School Finance Litigation

The issues in the early school finance cases were whether states could allocate more funds to poor school districts and whether states had the obligation to provide additional funds for the education of students with special needs. These court decisions have helped establish some generally accepted legal principles concerning the levying of taxes for education and permissible procedures for allocating state funds to local school districts. Some of the seminal cases are discussed below.

Sawyer v. Gilmore and Dean v. Coddington

Two early state court decisions helped to establish legal principles related to the financing of schools. The first was *Sawyer* v. *Gil-*

more (1912), which challenged the school finance system in Maine. The state constitution in Maine mandated that "all taxes upon real or personal estate assessed by authority of this state shall be apportioned and assessed equally according to the just value thereof." At issue was a statute that established a common school fund from a tax assessed on all real property in the state. The statute provided that one-third of the fund was to be redistributed to cities and towns based on the number of students, and two-thirds would be redistributed based upon the assessed valuation of property located within the cities and towns. The plaintiff in *Sawyer* did not question the manner of assessment and collection of the tax; the contested issue was how the funds were distributed. The plaintiff charged that the method of distribution was unconstitutional because of the one-third, two-thirds split, which gave the wealthier towns a larger proportion of state school funds. Sawyer argued that this unequal distribution resulted in an inferior education, which violated both the state constitution and the equal protection clause of the U.S. Constitution.

In deciding the case, the court distinguished between the constitutional restraints on taxation and the constitutional limitations on distribution, holding that the unequal funding did not violate either the Maine or the U.S. Constitutions. The court held that it is a legislative prerogative to construct different bases of distribution and that the practice is permissible "provided the purpose be the public welfare." *Sawyer* concluded that taxes are contributions "for the common good" and that "in order that taxation may be equal and uniform in the constitutional sense, it is not necessary that the benefits arising therefrom should be enjoyed by all the people in equal degree."

The second case, from South Dakota, *Dean* v. *Coddington* (1964), challenged an unequal school funding mechanism on the basis of that state's constitution, which requires that "all taxation shall be equal and uniform," and under the equal protection clause of the U.S. Constitution's 14th Amendment. The plaintiffs were taxpayers in a school district that did not maintain either an elementary or secondary school. Consequently, the district was not entitled to receive funds from a foundation formula program established by the legislature (Johns and Morphet 1975).

The purpose of the South Dakota foundation program was to use all appropriated or donated funds for purposes of "equalizing school opportunity." The legislature had prescribed sophisticated formulas for distributing state funds in an effort "to encourage improvement of education at the local level," but this school district was ineligible to receive funds since it had not operated a school during the previous year.

As in *Sawyer*, the *Dean* court distinguished taxation from distribution and held that neither constitutional provision required equal distribution. The court reasoned that the argument that the "uniform" statement of the state constitution required uniform distribution would be interpreting the constitution "as though it read – and all *expenditures* shall be equal and uniform." Citing several cases, the court held that "no requirements of uniformity or of equal protection of the law limit the power of a legislature in respect to allocation and distribution of public funds." While not indicating that it was applying an equal protection clause test, the court concluded that "the distribution of funds as directed in Ch. 77, Laws of 1963, is upon a reasonable basis of classification."

These two cases established the premise that a state could have an equalization program that resulted in the state taxing one district and giving the money to another district. The state payments are based on each district's need for funds as calculated by applying a uniform tax rate as the local share of the state's foundation program. Further, consistent with statutes, governmental agencies can distribute funds using such factors as the number of users, student attendance figures, assessed value of real property, or some other basis.

Brown v. Board of Education of Topeka

The landmark case of *Brown* v. *Board of Education of Topeka* (1954) provided the U.S. Supreme Court with the opportunity to rule definitively on whether public education is a constitutional right. Even though the Court did not directly address questions related to school funding, it did apply the equal protection clause, ruling that differences in access to an education are contrary to the principle of equal protection and thus are unconstitutional.

Linda Brown, an elementary school student in Topeka, Kansas, was required to attend an all-black school when an all-white school was located much closer to her home. A Kansas statute permitted, but did not require, cities with populations greater than 15,000 to maintain separate school facilities for black and white students. While other schools in the community were not segregated, the Topeka Board of Education operated segregated elementary schools.

Interpreting solely the equal protection clause of the U.S. Constitution, the Court held that public education is a constitutional right. Because "education is perhaps the most important function of state and local governments," educational "opportunity, where the state has undertaken to provide it, is a right which must be made available to all on equal terms."

The legal principle articulated in *Brown* brought renewed attention to the *Plessy* v. *Ferguson* (1896) decision, in which the Court had articulated the separate-but-equal doctrine, which provided that "equality of treatment is accorded when the races are provided substantially equal facilities, even though these facilities be separate." In *Brown*, the federal district court examined the "tangible" factors of education such as buildings, teacher salaries, and school curricula, and found them to be substantially equal. The Supreme Court, though, decided that qualities that could not be objectively measured prevented separate schools from being equal. The Court viewed such factors as opportunity to discuss and exchange views with other students and the feeling of inferiority that separate schools generate as critically important and held that "in the field of public education the doctrine of 'separate but equal' has no place. Separate educational facilities are inherently unequal. Therefore, . . . the plaintiffs . . . are, by reason of the segregation complained of, deprived of the equal protection of the laws guaranteed by the Fourteenth Amendment." The Court did not address the "suspect" nature of racial classifications; and it did not apply one of the three equal protection clause standards of analysis, leaving open the question of whether education, while certainly a constitutional right, would be considered a fundamental right entitled to strict scrutiny.

McInnis v. Shapiro and Burruss v. Wilkerson

The tendency for the courts to defer to the legislature in school funding issues was also evident in *McInnis* v. *Shapiro* (1968). In that case, a federal district court in Illinois addressed the question of whether unequal per-student expenditures in Illinois school districts violated the equal protection clause of the U.S. Constitution. The plaintiffs argued that public school expenditures should be based only on pupils' educational needs and stressed "the inequality inherent in having school funds partially determined by a pupil's place of residence."

The Illinois statutory scheme involved in *McInnis* included a per-pupil flat grant and an equalization grant calculated on the minimum assessed tax rate. The latter payment was received even when the assessed rate was greater than the minimum. When the local tax revenue generated by the minimum assessed rate plus the per-pupil flat grant was less than $400, the difference was made up by the equalization grant. Thus the flat grant plus the equalized grant guaranteed a base amount or foundation level of $400 per student. Although the equalization grant had been designed to compensate for variations in property value per pupil between districts, per-pupil expenditures still varied from $480 to $1,000.

The plaintiffs contended that 1) a strict scrutiny test under the equal protection clause should be applied, and 2) because education is so important to the nation's welfare, the courts should carefully examine state funding mechanisms designed to equalize per-pupil expenditures and invalidate them if less restrictive means are available. The concept of "least restrictive means" refers to the extent to which the funding mechanism accomplishes the state's purpose in the simplest manner. The plaintiffs also contended that "*only* a financing system which apportions public funds according to the educational needs of the students satisfies the Fourteenth Amendment." The court, noting that the plaintiffs had not provided a definition for "educational need," defined it as "a conclusory term, reflecting the interaction of several factors such as the quality of teachers, the students' potential, prior education, environmental and parental upbringing, and the school's physical plant."

In *McInnis*, the court declined to apply a strict scrutiny test, explaining, as did the courts in *Sawyer* and *Dean*, that the appropriation of public funds is a policy decision for the legislative branch of government rather than for a court sitting as a "super-legislature." The court's standard was apparently the rational basis test because it quoted the *McGowan* v. *Maryland* (1961) language that "the constitutional safeguard is offended only if the classification rests on grounds wholly irrelevant to the achievement of the State's objective." The court held that the school finance legislation at issue was not "arbitrary" and "where differences do exist from district to district, they can be explained rationally." While the court acknowledged the plaintiffs' concern over "the inequality inherent in having school funds partially determined by a pupil's place of residence," it indicated that the legislature had decided to allow local choice and to permit local citizens to select which municipal services, such as schools, police protection, or roads, they considered to be most valuable.

McInnis is especially noteworthy among school finance cases in that it refers to the absence of "judicially manageable standards" that a court could use to review the constitutionality of educational finance decisions. "The only possible standard is the rigid assumption that each pupil must receive the same dollar expenditures," and such a "single, simple formula" is impracticable because conditions vary throughout a state.

The *McInnis* decision expressly rejected the educational need argument, declaring, "there is no Constitutional requirement that public school expenditures be made only on the basis of pupils' educational needs without regard to the financial strength of local school districts." The court explained that "surely, quality education for all is more desirable than uniform, mediocre instruction. Yet if the Constitution only commands that all children be treated equally, the latter result would satisfy the Fourteenth Amendment." Thus, the court saw no constitutional defect in a state's practice of effectively conditioning a student's education quality on whether the student lived in a poor or affluent district, stating that "the inequality inherent in having school funds partially determined by a pupil's place of residence . . . is an inevitable consequence of decentralization." (The court was using the term "decentralization" here to describe the division of the state into separate school districts.)

In a similar case during the same period, *Burruss* v. *Wilkerson* (1969) addressed the claim that Virginia's school finance system did not account for different educational needs and therefore violated the equal protection clause of the U.S. Constitution and Virginia's constitutional provision requiring the General Assembly to "establish and maintain an efficient system of public free schools throughout the State." In Bath County, the lack of sufficient taxable property base resulted in it receiving less money for public education. Citing *McInnis*, the court held that "the courts have neither the knowledge, nor the means, nor the power to tailor the public moneys to fit the varying needs of these [underfunded] students throughout the State," but assured the plaintiffs that "The General Assembly undoubtedly will come to their relief."

These early school finance cases upheld state school funding mechanisms as lying within the purview of legislative authority. Most notably, this early litigation stage approved the concept of equalization in the distribution of funds but rejected any constitutionally based requirement that differences in educational need be recognized.

The Second Stage of School Finance Litigation

The 1970s marked the appearance of a new equal protection precedent in the continuing saga of educational finance litigation (Jordan and Alexander 1973). Both the California Supreme Court and the U.S. Supreme Court have squarely ruled on the questions of 1) whether public education is a fundamental right or a suspect classification and 2) what standard of review is to be applied in analyzing education funding methods. Key cases relating to these questions are discussed below.

Serrano v. Priest

A series of cases referred to as *Serrano* v. *Priest* (1971 to 1988) involved a constitutional challenge to California's statutory school funding system. *Serrano I*, the first in the series, was a review of a lower court order by the California Supreme Court. At the trial court level, the defendants, comprised of various state and county government officials, requested a dismissal of the case on the ground that none of the claims stated facts sufficient to constitute a cause of action. After the trial court dismissed the case, the plaintiffs appealed the dismissal to the state supreme court. Because the California Supreme Court was reviewing a dismissal order rather than hearing an appeal of a lower court decision, the court was required to assume that all facts set forth in the plaintiffs' complaint were true and then to determine whether those facts could properly form the basis for a legally recognized claim.

Thus *Serrano I* did not constitute a decision on the merits of the case. The California Supreme Court held that the facts did form the basis for a claim and remanded the case to the trial court with directions that the trial be allowed to proceed. The subsequent trial court decision was appealed to the Supreme Court in *Serrano II*.

In *Serrano I*, the plaintiffs alleged that the California school financing system was heavily dependent on local property taxes, which resulted in wide disparities in revenue available to different school districts. The plaintiffs claimed this constituted a violation of the equal protection clauses of both the U.S. and California Constitutions. The complaint specifically alleged that the financing scheme made the quality of education a function of the "wealth of the children's parents" and of the "geographical accident" of the school district in which the children resided, and failed to take into account the "variety of educational needs" of the children in the several school districts. The state had attempted to correct this inequity by providing a foundation program and a supplemental aid program to augment the local taxes. The foundation program was designed to guarantee that each district would have sufficient revenue to reach or exceed a minimum amount.

In its decision, the court first noted that it had previously construed certain provisions of the California Constitution to be equivalent to the equal protection clause of the 14th Amendment to the U.S. Constitution. It then explained the rational basis and strict scrutiny tests that were to be used in applying the equal protection clause to legislative classifications.

The court found it "irrefutable" that the California financing system classified districts on the basis of wealth, and that wealth, as measured by the assessed valuation of real property within a school district, was the major determinant of educational expenditures. The court noted that while "the amount of money raised locally is also a function of the rate at which the residents of a district are willing to tax themselves, as a practical matter districts with small tax bases simply cannot levy taxes at a rate sufficient to produce the revenue that more affluent districts reap with minimal tax efforts." Due to their large tax bases, affluent districts can provide a higher quality education for public school students while paying low tax rates and thus "can have their cake and eat it too," while poor districts "have no cake at all" due to their inability "to raise their taxes high enough to match the educational offerings of wealthier districts."

Serrano I then discussed education as a fundamental right. Citing *Brown*, the court described education as "a major determinant of an individual's chances for economic and social success in our competitive society," which has "a unique influence on a child's development as a citizen and his participation in political and community life."

The court then articulated five reasons supporting the treatment of education as a fundamental interest: 1) education is essential to "preserving an individual's opportunity to compete successfully in the economic marketplace, despite a disadvantaged background"; 2) while not everyone will require the services of a police or fire department, education is "universally relevant"; 3) few government

66

services have as extensive contact with the recipient as does education, which takes place over 10 to 13 years; 4) "education is unmatched in the extent to which it molds the personality of the youth of society"; and 5) "education is so important that the state has made it compulsory."

After classifying education as a fundamental right and finding that the state had not demonstrated that its funding system was necessary to the attainment of any compelling state interest, the case was remanded to the trial court, which then proceeded with a trial. Reading the language of *Serrano I* as an indication of how the state supreme court would ultimately rule on the merits of a school funding case, the California legislature amended the funding statutes; and the revised system was reviewed in 1976 in *Serrano II*.

A second development after *Serrano I* was the dramatic federal precedent set in the U.S. Supreme Court's decision in *Rodriguez*, which held that public education was not a fundamental right under the U.S. Constitution. As a result, the second *Serrano* court was faced with a different funding scheme and a directly relevant U.S. Supreme Court decision.

After *Serrano I*, the trial court heard the case on the merits and found the California school financing system unconstitutional. The defendants appealed, and the state supreme court affirmed in *Serrano II*. The California state legislature made two changes in its school funding system shortly after the *Serrano I* decision. First, it increased the minimum per-pupil amount guaranteed to each district. Second, it imposed limitations on maximum per-pupil expenditures in each school district exclusive of state and federal aid and of revenue gained from override taxes. According to the court, the new legislation "while significant, did not purport to alter the basic concept underlying the California public school financing system," which the court termed a "foundation approach" designed "to insure a certain guaranteed dollar amount for the education of each child in each school district, and to defer to the individual school district for the provision of whatever additional funds it deems necessary to the furtherance of its particular educational goals."

According to the court, the system as modified did not treat students equally: "Although an equal expenditure level per pupil in every district is not educationally sound or desirable because of differing educational needs, equality of educational opportunity requires that all school districts possess an equal ability in terms of revenue to

67

provide students with substantially equal opportunities for learning."
The court noted that "differences in dollars do produce differences
in pupil achievement" and held that "there is a distinct relationship
between cost and the quality of educational opportunities afforded."

Both *Serrano* cases were thoroughly researched and provided extremely articulate opinions, which exhaustively explain the court's
reasoning. Taken together, the texts of *Serrano I*, *Serrano II*, and
Rodriguez constitute perhaps the clearest examination of the application of equal protection analysis to school funding laws.

The *Serrano* cases illustrate a major disadvantage faced by the plaintiffs who seek to use the courts as a means for changing public policy: litigation takes an inordinate amount of time. While *Serrano* did
ultimately hold in plaintiffs' favor, the final decision took more than
seven years. Further, once a court holds a legislative scheme unconstitutional, subsequent legislation designed to rectify the problem also may need to be reviewed by a court to determine whether
it conforms to the earlier decision.

San Antonio Independent School District v. Rodriguez

Another landmark school funding case was *San Antonio Independent School District* v. *Rodriguez* (1973), which challenged the in-
terdistrict funding disparities in Texas under the equal protection
clause of the U.S. Constitution. Because the Texas system was similar
to those in many other states, *Rodriguez* presented the potential for
the U.S. Supreme Court to cause major restructuring of school funding
systems across the country. One indication of the importance of this
case is that 28 state attorneys general filed friend-of-the-court briefs
urging that the Court uphold the existing Texas funding system, which
had been declared unconstitutional by a lower court.

In Texas, total funds for schools were derived from state aid and
local taxation in approximately equal proportions. However, the state
foundation program was financed with approximately 80% from
general state revenues and 20% from local districts. The districts'
share, called the "Local Fund Assignment," was apportioned among
the 1,161 districts under an ability-to-pay formula. However, districts were allowed by law to impose a property tax at a rate higher
than that necessary to meet the Local Fund Assignment. Thus districts with a sufficient tax base and with voter approval had the authority to raise additional funds earmarked specifically for their own
schools.

The Court, in applying its established equal protection clause tests, first held that the plaintiffs had not adequately identified members of any disfavored class, intimating that "poor" should have been defined with reference to an "absolute or functional level of impecunity." Second, the Court explained that its past equal protection clause cases involved groups of individuals who had experienced absolute deprivations because of their complete inability to pay rather than groups who had experienced "disproportionate burdens." The Court distinguished *Rodriguez* as presenting an issue of receipt of a poorer quality education rather than an absolute deprivation of education and decided "at least where wealth is involved, the Equal Protection Clause does not require absolute equality or precisely equal advantages."

This decision is particularly noteworthy for its clear, negative rulings by the Court on the issues of whether wealth is a suspect class and whether public education is a fundamental right. The Court held that not only was the alleged affected class ill-defined and "amorphous," but also that both "the system of alleged discrimination and the class it defines have none of the traditional indicia of suspectness: the class is not saddled with such disabilities, or subjected to such a history of purposeful unequal treatment, or relegated to such a position of political powerlessness as to command extraordinary protection from the majoritarian political process."

While previous Court decisions may have applied a heightened level of scrutiny to a wealth classification, the *Rodriguez* decision explained that those cases involved some form of additional burden or discrimination and indicated that "this Court has never heretofore held that wealth discrimination alone provides an adequate basis for invoking strict scrutiny."

In dismissing the argument that public education is a fundamental right, the Court acknowledged its "historic dedication to public education" and its "abiding respect for the vital role of education in a free society." But the Court then indicated that its test for determining whether a right is fundamental requires an assessment as to whether the right is explicitly or implicitly guaranteed by the Constitution. The Court quoted from an earlier case, *Madden* v. *Kentucky* (1940): "The Court today does *not* 'pick out particular human activities, characterize them as "fundamental," and give them added protection. . . .' To the contrary, the Court simply recognizes, as it must, an established constitutional right, and gives to that right no less protection than the Constitution itself demands." *Rodriguez* ultimately held that education "is not among the rights afforded explicit protection under our Federal Constitution. Nor do we find any basis for saying it is implicitly so protected."

The plaintiffs asserted that education was so intertwined with speech as to require both to be treated as suspect classes. But according to the Court, there was no nexus between speech and education of such magnitude to require the treatment of education as a suspect class, explaining that the citizens' guarantee of free speech was not a guarantee of the most *effective* speech.

The Court added that it lacked the expertise and familiarity with local problems that would be required to resolve issues of taxation and appropriation. Questions of resource allocation are fields in which "legislatures possess the greatest freedom in classification."

After holding that no suspect class was involved and that public education does not constitute a fundamental right, the Court applied the rational basis test to the Texas school funding system. It concluded that the desire to promote local control was a sufficient and rational basis, overruled the district court, and upheld the constitutionality of the Texas system.

Robinson v. Cahill

A third prominent educational finance case from New Jersey was *Robinson* v. *Cahill* (1973 to 1976), which entailed seven separate opinions and orders by the New Jersey Supreme Court over a period of almost four years. In 1972 a New Jersey trial court examined the elementary and secondary school funding statutes and held that they violated the equal protection clauses of both the U.S. and New Jersey Constitutions. Of special significance in the New Jersey system was the high percentage of total school revenue coming from local taxation. In *Robinson*, the trial court found that 67% of the statewide total school operating expenses came from local ad valorem taxation of real property, 28% came from state appropriations, and 5% from federal aid. Because the state did not effectively equalize, a considerable disparity existed in the amount spent per pupil across districts. Thus the lower court held that the system unconstitutionally discriminated against students in low-wealth areas.

The New Jersey Supreme Court agreed that the system was unconstitutional, but for different reasons than those cited by the trial court. First, the New Jersey high court noted that the U.S. Supreme Court in *Rodriguez* had held that state funding mechanisms would be subject to the rational basis equal protection test. The New Jersey court ruled that the desire to grant local fiscal responsibility to local government constitutes a rational basis; and the court added that one of the consequences of this "home rule" is that local authorities will decide how much money will be raised for all local needs, including education.

According to the court, "statewide uniformity in expenditure" for education is not required, just as sums spent per resident for police and fire protection — services which are just as essential as education — may vary according to local decision. The court suggested that the New Jersey system also would meet a compelling state interest test by mentioning that "we find no decision of the United States Supreme Court holding that the State's interest in the institution of local government would not be 'compelling'. . ."

Second, in *Robinson* the court rejected the argument that education constituted a fundamental right. The court interpreted *Brown* as not elevating public education to this level. According to *Robinson*, the *Brown* decision involved a classification based on race that would have reached the same result regardless of the level of constitutional right involved.

What disturbed the New Jersey Supreme Court was the state constitutional provision requiring that "the Legislature shall provide for the maintenance and support of a thorough and efficient system of free public schools for the instruction of all the children in this State between the ages of five and eighteen years." Historically, New Jersey had at one time imposed a statewide school tax that was distributed on the basis of the number of eligible pupils. This system was modified in response to complaints that some districts were deliberately undervaluing their real property. In terms of dollar input per pupil, the court determined that the current system was not "thorough and efficient" and hence was unconstitutional. The court interpreted "thorough and efficient" in terms of dollars, because the legislature had not articulated adequate measures of educational opportunity to which the state constitution's "thorough and efficient" provision could be applied.

Calling the present New Jersey system a "patchy product reflecting provincial contests," the court held "the State must define in some discernible way the educational obligation and must *compel* the local school districts to raise the money necessary to provide that opportunity." The court also held that the constitution required, at a minimum, "that educational opportunity which is needed in the contemporary setting to equip a child for his role as a citizen and as a competitor in the labor market." And if a district could not provide the necessary funding, responsibility would fall on the state to provide the programs and facilities mandated by the constitution under the "thorough and efficient" clause. The court invited additional arguments as to whether it had the authority to alter existing legislative appropriations.

In *Robinson II*, the New Jersey Supreme Court held that it would not alter appropriations under the then-existing funding system unless the legislature failed to enact legislation in compliance with its *Robinson* decisions by 31 December 1974.

In *Robinson III*, after the legislature failed to enact appropriate legislation, the court elected not to disturb financing for the school year beginning 1 July 1975, but requested additional arguments with respect to court intervention in school funding for the 1976-77 school year. In *Robinson IV*, the New Jersey Supreme Court delineated a "contingent or provisional remedy" that reallocated educational funds for the 1976-77 year only.

The Public School Education Act of 1975 was enacted on 29 September 1975. This act revised the school funding system in an attempt to equalize school revenues across the state. Of particular importance was the act's grant of authority to the state to compel school districts to tax their property more heavily up to a cap restricting annual increases to a certain percentage over the prior year. The act also established standards for measuring substantive educational content.

Local districts were required to establish goals and objectives consistent with legislative guidelines, which included: 1) establishment of educational goals at both the state and local levels; 2) encouragement of public involvement in goal setting; 3) instruction intended to produce the attainment of reasonable levels of proficiency in the basic communications and computational skills; 4) a breadth of program offerings designed to develop the individual talents and abilities of pupils; 5) programs and supportive services for all pupils, especially those who are educationally disadvantaged or who have special educational needs; 6) adequately equipped, sanitary, and secure physical facilities and adequate materials and supplies; 7) qualified instructional and other personnel; 8) efficient administrative procedures; 9) an adequate state program of research and development; and 10) evaluation and monitoring programs at both the state and local levels.

In *Robinson V*, in light of the newly adopted measures of educational adequacy, the court shifted its focus from dollar disparity to educational content, vacated its reallocation order in *Robinson IV*, and held the new legislation to be constitutional if fully funded. In addition, *Robinson V* held that the "thorough and efficient" clause required at least a minimum level of educational expenditures. When the legislature did not provide sufficient funding, the court in *Robinson VI* enjoined New Jersey officials from expending funds for the support of schools except in such non-instructional financial categories as building maintenance, security, and bonds. On 9 July 1976, after further legislative action, *Robinson VII* in turn vacated the order in *Robinson VI* after the court was satisfied that the legislature had fully funded the Public School Education Act of 1975.

The *Robinson* cases present a striking example of legislation from the bench. Throughout the seven cases, there was considerable debate about whether a court has the power to order the reallocation of money appropriated by the legislature. Under the doctrine of separation of powers, appropriation is clearly the prerogative of the legislative branch. But in the New Jersey Supreme Court's view, when the legislature continued to act in an unconstitutional fashion in its educational appropriations, the court had an obligation to provide a remedy by enjoining the expenditure of appropriated funds. *Robinson* illustrates the potential reach of judicial power and serves to explain why state courts have continued to be used as mechanisms for seeking changes in state school funding systems.

Robinson is especially interesting for two reasons. First, the state funding system was held unconstitutional under a state constitutional provision relating to a "thorough and efficient" education rather than under an equal protection clause. Second, the details of the decision are more prescriptive in terms of remedies than typically found in other court decisions. Additionally, the New Jersey school funding litigation is significant because of the state's high per-pupil expenditures compared to those of the other states. The series of decisions in New Jersey and the continuing litigation in California and Texas also illustrate the tendency for litigation to continue over a period of years rather than being resolved quickly.

Municipal Overburden

The issue of underfunded schools as a result of municipal overburden, or a high tax burden for governmental functions other than education, was the major point of contention in *Board of Education, Levittown Union Free School District* v. *Nyquist* (1982). In the New York school funding system, schools located within municipalities receive their funding as part of the total municipal budgetary process. Thus schools must compete for funding with police, fire, health, housing, transportation, and other municipal services. Schools located outside municipalities also received funding through property taxes, but the range of public services supported by the total property tax bill is less in nonmunicipal areas.

Plaintiffs in *Levittown* alleged that, because the state statutory equalization formula did not reconcile the resulting revenue disparities between municipal and nonmunicipal districts, the statutes violated the equal protection clauses of both the New York and U.S. Constitutions as well as the state constitution's requirement that "the legislature shall provide for the maintenance and support of a system of free common schools, wherein all the children of this state may be educated."

The court rejected the federal equal protection claim by applying the *Rodriguez* rational basis test and held that promotion of local control over education constituted a rational basis for the funding scheme. The state equal protection claim was similarly rejected under a prior New York decision requiring rational basis as the standard for review for constitutional challenges to public education. Finally, the court denied the claim under the state constitution's education article, which it interpreted as requiring that every district provide only a minimal acceptable level of education, but not that education be equal across every district.

This series of state court cases established the concept of public education funding systems being subjected to the rational basis test. Even though the strict scrutiny test was not applied as a general principle, the California and New Jersey litigation illustrate that the interaction of judicial decisions with legislative actions tends to result in legislative responses, recurrent challenges, and continuing judicial review. This trend also is evident in the most recent Texas litigation discussed in the next section.

Recent Developments in Finance Litigation

While education funding was the focus of considerable court activity during the early 1970s, the number of cases declined until the mid-1980s. Recently, decisions have been handed down by the states' highest courts in New Jersey, Texas, Montana, and Kentucky. Action also has been initiated in about 20 states, including such diverse states as Alabama, Arizona, Idaho, Illinois, Kansas, Minnesota, Ohio, Pennsylvania, Tennessee, and Virginia. Some of the cases have not yet been heard at the trial court level, and rulings have not been handed down by the states' highest courts in others. These cases may signal a new trend in the thrust of the litigation, in that plaintiffs have sought to demonstrate the existence of inequitable treatment of students that contributes to disparity in educational opportunity.

With the clear directive from *Rodriguez* that education is not a fundamental right, and the risk that the *Rodriguez* interpretation may be applied by a state court to its own constitution's equal protection clause, litigants have recently sought legal redress under their state constitutions' education clauses. The clauses contain language providing for such objectives as "a general diffusion of knowledge" (Texas), "quality public schools" (Montana), and "efficiency" in education (Kentucky).

In 1985 school finance litigation emerged again in New Jersey. This time the New Jersey Public School Education Act was challenged as unconstitutional. In *Abbott* v. *Burke I* (1985) the New Jersey Supreme Court determined that the funding system implemented pursuant to the Public School Education Act should first be reviewed through administrative channels before the judicial system could rule on alleged constitutional problems.

After applicable administrative remedies were exhausted, the New Jersey Supreme Court issued its ninth decision on the state's school funding scheme in *Abbott* v. *Burke II* (1990). In this most recent challenge, the plaintiffs were students in schools located in poor districts, who argued that the funding scheme under the Public School Education Act had not resulted in a "thorough and efficient" education for all New Jersey students. With the state contributing only 40% of all school operating costs, the majority of school funding was derived from local property taxes, which resulted in a considerable funding disparity between high-wealth and low-wealth districts.

In *Abbott II*, the court distinguished its ninth look at the New Jersey funding scheme from the many school funding cases in other states, noting that "none has the unique attribute of this case: an educational funding system specifically designed to conform to a prior court decision, having been declared constitutional by the Court but now attacked as having failed to achieve the constitutional goal. In short, we are the only state involved in a second round on this issue."

In a 56-page opinion that traced the full history of the *Robinson/Abbott* saga, the court declared the funding scheme unconstitutional as applied to poor school districts only. Restricting its decision again to an interpretation of the "thorough and efficient" clause of the state constitution, the court reasoned that poor districts in New Jersey were so substantially underfunded and underequipped as compared to wealthy districts in the state that a "constitutional failure of education" existed in New Jersey "no matter what test is applied to determine thorough and efficient." Further, because the system in the poor districts was not able to equip its students "to fulfill their roles as citizens and competitors in the market," the legislative funding scheme did not meet the *Robinson I* definition of "thorough and efficient."

The court's ruling touched on four points: "1) the [Public School Education] Act must be amended to assure funding of education in poorer urban districts at the level of property-rich districts, 2) such funding cannot be allowed to depend on the ability of local school districts to tax, 3) such funding must be guaranteed and mandated by the State, and 4) the level of funding must also be adequate to provide for the special educational needs of these poorer urban districts in order to redress their extreme disadvantages." The court declined to specify a new scheme for the legislature to enact, electing to allow it the discretion to devise any remedy it felt appropriate to meet the standards for the funding system detailed in the court's latest decision.

Abbott II discussed at length the purported relationship between funding and quality of education. The court noted that "While it is possible that the richest of education can be conferred in the rudest of surroundings, the record in this case demonstrates that deficient facilities are conducive to a deficient education." The judges were obviously shocked by the crumbling conditions of New Jersey's inner-city public schools. While the judges conceded that "obviously, we are no more able to identify what these disadvantaged students need in concrete educational terms than are the experts," they nevertheless concluded that "what they don't need is more disadvantage, in the form of a school district that does not even approach the funding level that supports advantaged students . . . the law entitles them to more." And they added, "even if not a cure, money will help, and . . . these students are constitutionally entitled to that help," and "all suspect . . . that if the children of poorer districts went to school today in richer ones, educationally they would be a lot better off."

The court's ruling indicated that many decisions made in the field of education "are based on the premise that what money buys affects the quality of education," listing as examples the regular practice of school boards to attempt to increase their budgets for the purpose of improving the education provided in their districts, the numerous special programs that are accompanied by grant funds, the state-aid program itself, and the state's power to require local districts to increase their budgets.

In 1989 the Texas Supreme Court ruled in the case of *Edgewood Independent School District* v. *Kirby*. This case involved an interpretation of Article VII, Section 1 of the Texas Constitution, which provided that "general diffusion of knowledge being essential to the preservation of the liberties and rights of the people, it shall be the duty of the Legislature of the State to establish and make suitable provision for the support and maintenance of an efficient system of public free schools."

In Texas, local property taxes were providing 50% of school funds and the state was providing 42%. But the differences in property values were so great that the wealthiest district had more than $14 million of property wealth per student while the poorest had only $20,000, reflecting a 700 to 1 ratio.

The court decided "general diffusion of knowledge" meant knowledge spread statewide. Noting that the legislature's responsibility to support education as opposed to other public interests is different because it is constitutionally imposed, the *Edgewood* court held that the funding scheme was unconstitutional because it resulted in education "that is limited and unbalanced" rather than "a diffusion [of education] that is general." The court also ruled that "districts must have substantially equal access to similar revenues per pupil at similar levels of tax effort" and dismissed the argument that school finance reform would result in the elimination of local control. The Texas Supreme Court has made two additional rulings, and the case is unresolved in 1992.

In Montana, the legislature enacted a law requiring each county to levy a 40-mill tax on all property in the state. If the revenue generated from this tax exceeded the amount necessary to fund the foundation program in that county, the surplus was to be remitted to the state to be used as state equalization aid. In *State ex rel. Woodahl* v. *Straub* (1974), the court held the tax to be constitutional, even though the amounts generated by some districts exceeded the amount returned to those districts, by using the reasoning that, taken as a whole, the system was "a rational method to accomplish the goal of equal educational opportunity for each person of the state."

Later, in *Helena Elementary School District No. 1* v. *State* (1989), the court, without mentioning *Woodahl*, held the Montana funding scheme unconstitutional under the state constitutional provision requiring an equitable distribution of the state's share of the cost of "a basic system of free quality public elementary and secondary schools." Because the major portion of school funding came from the state foundation program and the legislature had inadequately funded the program, districts had been relying excessively on voted and permissive levies. Thus wealthy districts were better funded than poor districts, which violated the state constitution's requirement of equitable funding.

Defining "efficient" was the major task faced by the Kentucky Supreme Court in *Rose* v. *Council for Better Education, Inc.* (1989). In a broad decision for the plaintiffs that declared the entire education system in Kentucky unconstitutional, the court interpreted the state constitutional provision requiring "an efficient system of common schools throughout the state" as one that possessed several characteristics: the system should make common schools free and available to all Kentucky children, should be substantially uniform throughout the state, should provide equal educational opportunities to all students regardless of those students' economic circumstances or places of residence, and should receive sufficient legislative funding to enable it to provide each Kentucky child an adequate education. By articulating only these general goals, the court declined to direct the legislature to enact specific statutes or to raise taxes in order to make the Kentucky system conform to the court's interpretation of the constitutional mandate. Thus the court provided little guidance as to constitutionally sound remedial measures. However, the court's decision did prod the Kentucky legislature to enact sweeping reforms.

Conclusions

Judicial activism in school finance undoubtedly will continue through the 1990s. Recent challenges to state school finance systems appear to have succeeded because the plaintiffs have refined the strategy of emphasizing that the existing systems have resulted in students not having equal access to educational opportunities. Although past cases show that these differences in access to educational programs can be demonstrated convincingly, the courts will not necessarily prescribe action, often preferring to defer to state legislatures and individual school districts to address and correct the disparities.

In reviewing court rulings, people often misinterpret state-level judicial decisions by placing excessive reliance on the wording of the decisions without considering the background issues and facts of the case, the applicable statutory and constitutional doctrines, and the legal and socio-political context within which the cases were litigated. Careful analysis of precedent is especially critical because current cases are being rendered by the high courts in individual states on the basis of the particular constitutional provisions in that state.

The recent successful challenges to state school finance plans in Kentucky, Montana, New Jersey, and Texas may inspire other litigants. In some sense, these more recent cases are based on a broader set of assumptions about indicators of inequities among school districts. The focus has been on such items as textbooks, instructional materials, course offerings, and instructional equipment. The primary focus of recent challenges to state school finance systems has been the alleged inequity in funding for the day-to-day operation of schools.

The next wave of school finance litigation may well include equity questions related to the ways in which differences in school facilities result in unfair treatment of students or in differences in taxpayer burden among school districts for capital outlay and debt service. Plaintiffs may seek to demonstrate that the disparity in taxable wealth among local school districts contributes to inequities in student access to facilities in the same manner as inequities in student access to educational programs. Courts may have to consider that many districts do not have sufficient bonding power to generate the funds required to provide needed school facilities. The courts will be handicapped to some extent because case law precedents on the school facilities issue are limited.

Efforts to provide judicial relief in the school facilities area will be complicated because of several difficult and complex questions. For example, should funding for school facilities be limited to those districts with debt service obligations? Should the state adopt school construction standards? Should local school districts have the power to issue bonds to finance construction of schools or should the state issue the bonds? Should state funds for school construction be integrated into or be separate from the basic school support program? Should a state agency be created to make grants or loans to low-wealth districts with the need for facilities?

Using the courts to achieve equity in state school finance systems can be characterized as a continuing but unattainable quest. The ongoing litigation in California, New Jersey, and Texas illustrates the lack of absolute measurable standards that can be imposed by courts or used by legislatures in evaluating various funding proposals. Given the decentralized nature of America's schools, state funding systems are not sufficiently refined to ensure sufficient funds for every child in every classroom. The resulting diversity may be both the greatest strength and greatest weakness of our public schools. And the unfairness of that diversity will be a continuing subject of litigation. The quest for equity likely will continue as long as the nation's schools are administered through 15,000 local school districts, which operate 80,000 individual schools, and as long as these districts have some discretionary spending and operational authority over such items as teacher salaries, course offerings, and instructional materials and equipment.

References

Johns, R.L., and Morphet, E.L. *The Economics and Financing of Education: A Systems Approach*. Englewood Cliffs, N.J.: Prentice-Hall, 1975.

Jordan, K.F., and Alexander, K. "Constitutional Methods of Financing Public Schools." In *Constitutional Reform of School Finance*, edited by K. Alexander and K.F. Jordan. Cambridge, Mass.: Lexington Books, 1973.

LaMorte, M.S. "Courts Continue to Address the Wealth Disparity Issue." *Educational Evaluation and Policy Analysis* 11, no. 1 (1989): 3-16.

Nowak, J.E., and Rotunda, R.D. *Constitutional Law*, Section 14.8. St. Paul, Minn.: West, 1991.

Odden, A.R., and Picus, L.O. *School Finance: A Policy Perspective*. New York: McGraw-Hill, 1992.

Webb, L.D.; McCarthy, M.; and Thomas, S. *Financing Elementary and Secondary Education*. Columbus, Ohio: Merrill, 1988.

Wright, C.A. *The Law of Federal Courts*. 4th ed. St. Paul, Minn.: West, 1983.

Table of Cases

 **CHAPTER 6**

Taxation and Sources of Revenues for Schools

The concept of general taxation to support the public schools is an American tradition dating from Colonial times. As a governmental function, public elementary and secondary education is financed with tax receipts rather than with tuition or fees. The direct beneficiaries of schools, students, do not have income. Since school attendance is compulsory, the charging of a fee would be discriminatory for poor and disadvantaged youth. Justifications for a tax-supported system of education include social equity, economic growth and development, and survival of the political system. Moreover, the benefits of an educated populace extend over generations and accrue to virtually all citizens. Thus providing revenues to support the public schools has come to be an accepted responsibility of government.

Taxation systems have effects beyond the raising of revenues. They need to be evaluated in terms of their overall impact on social, political, and economic conditions. In this chapter, four criteria are provided for evaluating the tax structure of a governmental unit (Due 1970).

Criteria for Evaluating a Taxation System

First, a tax should not cause economic distortions. The taxation system should not encourage consumers to make purchasing decisions that favor one essential good over another or one geographical area over another. Neither should a taxation system encourage businesses to select sites or choose production methods that favor one geographical area over another. Further, a taxation system should not influence a person's willingness to work and be productive in the national economy.

If a taxation system is to avoid undesirable economic consequences, it must be neutral; that is, one cannot escape the tax by changing one's place of residence or by not purchasing selective items that are taxed. No tax that generates large amounts of revenue is completely neutral, but the neutrality increases with the breadth and uniformity of coverage. For example, a general sales tax is more neutral than a selective sales tax on tobacco, gasoline, or alcohol. However, most taxes exclude some items and, therefore, are not neutral.

Second, a tax should be equitable for persons in the same relative circumstances. One view on tax equity is that it should be benefits-based, with the tax burden on an individual roughly proportional to the benefits received. Taxes for public schools are not benefits-based immediately or directly, since the benefits of education are spread among individuals and society in general and extend over generations.

A second view on tax equity is the ability to pay. This view is the one most commonly applied on the assumption that the general citizenry benefits from the public services supported by taxation. Income is the most commonly used indicator of ability to pay; other indicators are property ownership and consumption expenditures. The equity measure is the percentage of income that is paid in taxes.

Taxes can be classified as progressive, regressive, or proportional. Under a progressive tax, the tax rate increases as the taxpayer's ability to pay increases; that is, those with higher incomes pay a higher proportion of their income in taxes than do those with lesser incomes. Under a regressive tax system, taxpayers with lower incomes pay a higher proportion of their income in taxes. Under a proportional tax system, taxes are applied at a constant rate; for example, a fixed sales tax on goods and services is paid by all persons irrespective of their income level. Still another category is those taxes that are designed to discourage certain behaviors or consumptions, such as the so-called "sin taxes" on alcohol and tobacco.

Third, the rate of compliance with the tax should be high, with a minimum cost for enforcement and a reasonable cost for collection and administration. This criterion assumes that the tax will be difficult to evade and will not have loopholes that operate to the benefit of certain groups of taxpayers.

Fourth, the revenues generated by the taxation system should respond to the changes in the economy. Under this criterion of revenue elasticity, the revenue yield from the taxing system will rise proportionally without increasing rates during periods of inflation when governmental expenditures are increasing. However, the reverse generally is not acceptable to governmental units; that is, the tax yield will decline during a period of recession. That may be the time when the need for governmental spending is greatest.

In the following discussion of revenue sources for schools, each source is discussed briefly and then evaluated in terms of the criteria presented above.

Local Revenue Sources — Property Tax

The principal source of local revenue for schools is the ad valorem tax on real property. Classifications of real property include land, residences, apartment buildings, commercial buildings, railroads, and utilities. On the average, more that 90% of local tax revenues for public elementary and secondary schools comes from taxes on real property.

As a tax source, the property tax fails to meet some of the above criteria for evaluating a taxation system. Variations in property wealth and differences in tax rates among taxing jurisdictions tend to create economic distortions. Businesses may choose to locate in areas with lower property taxes, thus giving citizens who reside in those areas easier access to the businesses. Also, homes in a low-tax area may sell more easily than those in a high-tax area.

The equity of the property tax is a matter of debate. Advocates of the property tax say it is equitable because it discourages the hoarding of property and the concentration of property wealth in the hands of a few citizens. Critics of the property tax say it puts a burden on fixed-income taxpayers, whose residences are increasing in value resulting in higher taxes while their incomes remain the same. In such cases, the property tax is considered to be regressive because the heaviest tax burden falls on citizens with the least ability to pay. Another criticism is that, in some jurisdictions, certain types of property are assessed at different rates for tax-paying purposes.

Compliance rates for payment of the property tax are reasonably high, because failure to pay can result in forfeit of the property. However, the costs of administering and collecting property taxes are much higher than for either sales or income taxes. Property assessment is a major administrative cost, and maintenance of records and tax collection also require a substantial bureaucracy. Thus the property tax does not fare well on the criteria related to a minimum cost for enforcement and a reasonable cost for collection.

Although property taxes do not respond quickly to changes in the economy, they do have the advantage of being more stable than sales

84

and income taxes. Property tax revenue can be projected with reasonable accuracy for a budget year, whereas sales tax revenues are immediately responsive to shifts in the economy. Income taxes are only slightly more stable than sales taxes. In 1988-89, property taxes accounted for about 74% of local tax revenues for all governmental services (Bureau of the Census 1990).

Even though the local property tax is a major source of revenue for schools, taxpayer resistance often is high. Whereas sales taxes are paid in small amounts with each purchase made and income taxes typically are paid through payroll deductions, property taxes usually are paid annually or semi-annually upon receipt of the tax bill. This administrative procedure likely has contributed to increased taxpayer resistance to the property tax.

Inflationary pressures have an impact on the property tax in different ways. Double-digit inflation in the 1970s and early 1980s resulted in significant increases in the assessed value of property and in the costs for governmental services such as education. The result was large increases in property tax bills. Even though personal income may have risen at approximately the same rates as the assessed value of property, taxpayers tend to pay more attention to the amount of their tax bill than they do to the proportion of their income they spend on property taxes.

Retirees and others on fixed incomes worry that rising assessed values and higher tax bills will consume an increasing portion of their income. Their concern is that their property taxes may reach the confiscatory level and force them to sell their homes. Some states have provided relief for fixed-income taxpayers through a "circuit breaker" mechanism when property taxes exceed specified limits in relation to household income. Such programs can be administered as a tax credit or rebate in the state income tax.

From the state's perspective, a major concern in providing equity among school districts is the wide variation in assessment practices among local school districts. The problem is two-fold. First, the market value of a property can be determined only when the property is sold. If property is not sold, assessed values are frequently out of date. Second, many taxing jurisdictions do not use professional assessors, and their assessment procedures and standards may vary. Thus taxpayers living in houses with equal market values may receive tax bills for quite different amounts because of differences in assessment practices.

State Revenue Sources — Sales and Income Taxes

The principal sources of state revenues for schools are taxes on retail sales and services and on personal and corporate income. In 1988-89, sales tax revenues accounted for 49% of state revenues; and state personal and corporate income tax revenues accounted for 39% of state tax revenues (Bureau of the Census 1990). Both sales and income taxes fail to meet several criteria used in evaluating a taxation system.

All states have either sales or income taxes; the majority have both. The choices of where to live and to purchase goods and services tend to create economic distortions. Individuals may choose to locate in states without personal income taxes. Persons in a sales tax state but residing near the border of a state with no sales tax may elect to make their purchases across the border to escape the sales tax. Thus the taxing structure influences people to alter their behavior in order to take advantage of low-tax options.

The general retail sales tax is an American invention and is a major producer of state revenue in 90% of the states. Revenues from this tax typically are used to support a variety of state functions, including the public schools. Public resistance to the tax is low because it is paid in small amounts at the time of purchase, and adjustments can be made to protect low-income households.

One of the attractive features of the sales tax is the ability of the taxing jurisdiction to export some of the tax burden to non-residents, who pay the tax when they shop, eat, or lodge in the jurisdiction. Promoting tourism is one means to export the sales tax; another is to build large shopping malls that draw customers from other taxing jurisdictions.

A variety of adjustments or exemptions can be made to increase the equity of the sales tax. Exemptions may be granted for such necessities as groceries, essential basic clothing, and medical prescriptions. The merits of exempting necessities are often debated because of lost revenues and the range in expenditures among consumers. For example, with a full exemption for groceries, both the poor person's peanut butter and the rich person's caviar are exempted.

Procedures for relieving the sales tax burden on low-income persons have been developed. Credits for sales taxes paid can be applied against the state income tax, or a portion of the sales tax can be refunded directly to the eligible low-income taxpayer. The income tax credit/refund method is relatively easy to administer and does not result in significant losses in revenues; however, the low-income person must complete the state income tax form in order to receive the refunds.

Without some type of exemptions, rebates, or credits, the sales tax is considered to be regressive, or less equitable, because it puts a heavier burden on those with the least ability to pay. For example, low-income persons will pay a larger proportion of their income in the form of sales taxes than high-income persons.

The equity issue with regard to the state income tax is quite a different scenario. Most state income taxes have a varying rate structure in which the rate increases as a person's income increases. The income tax is considered to be more equitable because it is progressive.

Compliance rates for payment of state income and sales taxes are subject to interpretation. State income tax systems often use the administrative system of the federal income tax, and questions have long been raised about the overall compliance rates for the federal income tax. When significant changes are made in the federal income tax structure, states may find it necessary to adjust their systems accordingly because of the linkages between exemptions and rates in state and federal income taxes.

Compliance with the sales tax can be more easily monitored because payments are made at the point of purchase, and retail establishments can be identified and policed. Even though both sales and income taxes require an administrative bureaucracy, the costs of administering and collecting either tax are much less than for the property tax. Enforcement problems may be encountered, but sales and income taxes do fare well on the criteria related to a minimum cost for enforcement and a reasonable cost for collection.

Both sales and income taxes are quickly responsive to changes in the economy. Income from either will rise and fall with the economy. Compared to property taxes, sales and income taxes may not have the level of stability desired to permit sound fiscal planning, because revenue receipts can shift within a tax year if economic predictions are not correct. However, the combination of sales and income taxes with the property tax has considerable merit because the joint system has a mix of the desired qualities of stability and responsiveness.

Federal Revenue Sources — Income Tax

Federal funding for elementary and secondary education has always been limited, currently accounting for only about 6% of the total expenditure for K-12 education. The principal source of federal revenue for education is the federal income tax. In 1988-89, about 89% all federal government revenues came from corporate and personal income taxes (Bureau of the Census 1990).

A major advantage of the federal income tax is that its revenue-raising potential relies upon the entire nation as the tax base. Because the tax is collected throughout the nation, the possibility of creating economic distortions through collections is minimized. However, economic distortions can be created through exemptions used to discourage or encourage certain economic behavior by taxpayers, such as interest on installment purchases or home mortgage payments.

The federal income tax is considered to be equitable because of its progressive rate structure, even though that structure became less progressive with the federal tax reform legislation of 1984 and 1986. Nevertheless, rates continue to increase as a person's income increases, with higher-income persons paying a higher rate.

Compliance rates for payment of the federal income tax are of some concern, but the Internal Revenue Service has established a complex, computer-based system of reporting to increase collections and make enforcement easier. Even though the federal income tax requires a large bureaucracy, the costs of administering and collecting this tax are proportionally much less than for any other tax. The federal income tax fares well on the compliance criterion because of its relatively low cost for enforcement and collection.

The federal income tax is a more stable revenue source than state sales and income taxes because of its national economic base. However, revenues from the tax do respond to changes in the national economy, such as the unemployment rate. The federal income tax ranks second to the property tax as a stable source of revenue, but it has greater elasticity.

No single tax is the perfect solution to funding schools. The optimal taxation system consists of a balance between stability and responsiveness, has a progressive rate structure, and does not place an unfair burden on any group of taxpayers or encourage economic distortions.

Local School District Expenditure Patterns

Public elementary and secondary schools are labor-intensive endeavors. Personnel costs represent the majority of expenditures in local school budgets, with more than 75% of the typical school district's budget going for employee salaries and fringe benefits. Questions often are raised about the amount spent for administrator salaries at both the central office and the building level; typically these expenditures account for less than 10% of the total budget.

The percent of the budget allocated for various functions in the typical local school district for 1990-91 is shown in Table 6.1. These data are gathered from a national sample of school districts that participate in the Educational Research Service data system (Robinson and Protheroe 1991).

A somewhat different classification of data on local district expenditures was reported by the U.S. Department of Education (Snyder 1990). Comprehensive data collected from all school districts indicate that 61% of current expenditures goes for instruction, 4.8% for administration, 11.2% for plant operation, 12.3% for fixed charges,

Table 6.1. Average percent of total current expenditures by functional category.

Function	Percent of Budget*
Regular Classroom Instruction	50.4
Special Education Instruction/Services	8.2
Maintenance and Operations	8.2
School Site Leadership	5.5
Pupil Transportation	4.6
Auxiliary Instructional Services	4.1
Books and Materials	2.9
Other Current Expenditures	2.9
Environmental Conditioning	2.8
Central and Business Services	2.4
Executive Administration	1.9
Health and Attendance	1.5
Instructional Improvement	1.4
Other Instructional Services	1.1
Student Activities	1.0
Board of Education	0.6
Food Services	0.3
Other Student Services	0.2

Source: Robinson, G.E., and Protheroe, N., "Local School Budget Profiles Study," *School Business Affairs*, 57, no. 9 (1991): 8.

*Percents do not total to 100 percent because of rounding.

and 10.7% for other school services. The "instruction" category includes salaries for teachers, aides, librarians and media personnel, building-level administrators and other support staff, and instructional supplies and materials. Administration includes district-level items such as school board expenses, superintendent and other central office personnel, payroll and purchasing, staff development, curriculum development, and psychological services. Plant operation includes maintenance and custodial services and related supplies. Fixed charges include fringe benefits for employees and insurance. Pupil transportation expenditures are included in other school services.

State Support for Public Education

States vary greatly in their support for public education. In school year 1990-91, per-pupil expenditures for current operations (excluding school construction and retirement of debt) ranged from $8,455 in Connecticut to $2,767 in Utah. Per-pupil expenditure exceeded $8,000 in Connecticut, the District of Columbia, New Jersey, and New York. In 10 states, per-pupil expenditure averaged less than $4,000; and in 10 states the average per-pupil expenditure was greater than $6,000. The 1990-91 national average per-pupil expenditure was $5,208 per pupil in ADA (National Education Association 1991). Data for each state are presented in Table 6.2.

Historical data in Table 6.3 illustrate the growth in spending per pupil over the past 70 years. In 1989-90 dollars, per-pupil expenditures increased from $355 in 1919-20 to $4,848 in 1989-90. In adjusted dollars, the growth appears to be more dramatic; but the effect of inflation is illustrated in the constant dollars.

In 1990-91 the range in average teacher salaries by state was not as great as the range in average per-pupil expenditures. Data in Table 6.4 indicate that the lowest state average salary was in South Dakota at $22,363. The state average salaries below $25,000 were in Arkansas, Mississippi, North Dakota, and Oklahoma. The highest average salary was in Alaska at $43,861. The average salaries also were above $40,000 in Connecticut, District of Columbia, and New York. The national average was $33,015.

Among the states, differences in the proportion of revenues from various sources result from the interaction of several factors: tradition, community values, school district organizational patterns, concentrations of students from low-income families, federal ownership of land within the state, and differences in state economies.

Table 6.2. Current expenditures per pupil in average daily attendance, 1990-91.

State	Current Expenditure Per Pupil
50 States and D.C.	$5,208
Alabama	3,648
Alaska	6,952
Arizona	4,196
Arkansas	3,419
California	4,826
Colorado	4,702
Connecticut	8,455
Delaware	6,016
District of Columbia	8,221
Florida	5,003
Georgia	4,852
Hawaii	5,008
Idaho	3,211
Illinois	5,062
Indiana	4,398
Iowa	4,877
Kansas	5,044
Kentucky	4,390
Louisiana	4,041
Maine	5,894
Maryland	6,184
Massachusetts	6,351
Michigan	5,257
Minnesota	5,360
Mississippi	3,322
Missouri	4,479
Montana	4,794
Nebraska	4,080
Nevada	4,677
New Hampshire	5,474
New Jersey	8,451
New Mexico	4,446
New York	8,680
North Carolina	4,635
North Dakota	3,685
Ohio	5,269
Oklahoma	3,835
Oregon	5,291
Pennsylvania	6,534
Rhode Island	6,989
South Carolina	3,843
South Dakota	3,730
Tennessee	3,707
Texas	4,329
Utah	2,767
Vermont	5,740
Virginia	5,335
Washington	5,042
West Virginia	4,695
Wisconsin	5,946
Wyoming	5,255

Source: National Education Association, *Estimates of School Statistics, 1990-91* (Washington, D.C., 1991). Table 11, p. 39.

Table 6.3. National average expenditures per pupil in average daily attendance: 1919-20 to 1989-90.

Year	Unadjusted Dollars	Constant Dollars
1919-20	$ 53	$ 355
1929-30	87	643
1939-40	88	800
1949-50	210	1,128
1959-60	375	1,621
1969-70	816	2,743
1979-80	2,272	3,716
1989-90	4,848	4,848

Source: Snyder, T.D., *Digest of Education Statistics* (Washington, D.C.: National Center for Education Statistics, U.S. Department of Education, 1990). Table 154, p. 155.

As indicated in Table 6.5, the relative proportion of revenues from each level of government varies among states. For 1990-91 the national average was 44.5% from local sources, 49.3% from state sources, and 6.2% from federal sources. The state receiving the highest proportion of revenues from local sources was New Hampshire at 90.3%. Excluding Hawaii and the District of Columbia, which are single school districts, the state with the lowest proportion of revenues from local sources was New Mexico at 11.9%. Other states with 60% or more from local revenue sources are Michigan, Oregon, South Dakota, and Virginia.

For state sources of funds, other than the District of Columbia and Hawaii, the state receiving the highest proportion of revenues from state sources was New Mexico at 76.2%, and the lowest was New Hampshire at 7.3%. States receiving 60% or more of their revenues from state sources were Alabama, California, Delaware, Georgia, Idaho, Kentucky, North Carolina, Washington, and West Virginia.

For federal revenue sources, the high state was Mississippi at 15.5%, and the low state was New Hampshire at 2.4%. Other states receiving 10% or more of their revenue from federal sources were Alabama, Alaska, New Mexico, and South Dakota.

Among the 50 states, the estimated number of pupils in average daily attendance (ADA) in 1987 ranged from 4,978,018 in California and 3,107,760 in Texas to 92,500 in Delaware and 88,266 in

Table 6.4. Average annual salary of classroom teachers: 1990-91.

State	Average Annual Salary
50 States and D.C.	$33,015
Alabama	27,300
Alaska	43,861
Arizona	30,780
Arkansas	23,040
California	39,598
Colorado	32,020
Connecticut	43,847
Delaware	35,200
District of Columbia	42,288
Florida	30,387
Georgia	28,855
Hawaii	32,541
Idaho	25,485
Illinois	34,729
Indiana	32,178
Iowa	27,949
Kansas	29,923
Kentucky	29,089
Louisiana	26,240
Maine	28,700
Maryland	38,806
Massachusetts	36,090
Michigan	37,682
Minnesota	33,284
Mississippi	24,443
Missouri	28,607
Montana	26,210
Nebraska	26,592
Nevada	32,209
New Hampshire	31,329
New Jersey	38,790
New Mexico	26,194
New York	41,600
North Carolina	29,082
North Dakota	23,578
Ohio	32,615
Oklahoma	24,649
Oregon	32,200
Pennsylvania	35,471
Rhode Island	37,674
South Carolina	28,174
South Dakota	22,363
Tennessee	28,248
Texas	28,321
Utah	25,415
Vermont	30,986
Virginia	32,382
Washington	32,975
West Virginia	25,958
Wisconsin	33,100
Wyoming	28,988

Source: National Education Association, *Estimates of School Statistics, 1990-91* (Washington, D.C., 1991). Table 7, p. 35.

Table 6.5. Percentage distribution of revenues by source: 1990-91.

State	Federal	State	Local
50 States and D.C.	6.2	49.3	44.5
Alabama	12.6	68.1	19.3
Alaska	10.2	59.3	30.5
Arizona	5.0	43.2	51.7
Arkansas	9.5	58.7	31.8
California	7.2	67.4	25.4
Colorado	5.5	39.9	54.6
Connecticut	3.7	45.9	50.4
Delaware	7.9	66.1	25.9
District of Columbia	9.3	——	90.7
Florida	5.8	53.6	40.6
Georgia	6.4	61.2	32.4
Hawaii	8.7	91.2	0.1
Idaho	7.3	60.4	32.8
Illinois	7.4	36.8	55.9
Indiana	4.6	59.9	35.5
Iowa	5.3	51.6	43.1
Kansas	5.1	43.3	51.6
Kentucky	8.4	70.4	21.2
Louisiana	9.5	52.6	37.9
Maine	6.0	53.3	40.7
Maryland	4.9	38.3	56.8
Massachusetts	5.2	36.9	58.0
Michigan	4.5	35.4	60.0
Minnesota	4.4	53.8	41.8
Mississippi	15.5	54.9	29.6
Missouri	5.5	37.7	56.8
Montana	8.8	56.8	34.3
Nebraska	5.5	23.5	71.0
Nevada	3.7	37.7	58.6
New Hampshire	2.4	7.3	90.3
New Jersey	3.8	41.5	54.7
New Mexico	11.9	76.2	11.9
New York	5.2	43.2	51.6
North Carolina	6.1	66.4	27.5
North Dakota	7.5	48.2	44.3
Ohio	5.3	43.4	51.4
Oklahoma	7.5	48.2	44.3
Oregon	6.0	26.7	67.2
Pennsylvania	5.2	43.5	51.3
Rhode Island	4.0	44.2	51.8
South Carolina	8.0	51.7	40.3
South Dakota	10.5	25.7	63.8
Tennessee	9.5	48.0	42.6
Texas	7.9	43.1	49.0
Utah	6.7	56.5	36.9
Vermont	5.0	37.0	58.0
Virginia	4.6	34.6	60.8
Washington	5.5	73.9	20.6
West Virginia	7.8	65.4	26.8
Wisconsin	3.8	40.9	55.3
Wyoming	5.2	53.4	41.4

Source: National Education Association, *Estimates of School Statistics, 1990-91* (Washington, D.C., 1991). Table 9, p. 37.

Vermont. The 10 states with more than 1,000,000 pupils in ADA accounted for more than 50% of the total pupils. Data for each state are presented in Table 6.6.

As shown in Table 6.6, these 38,000,000 students were attending schools in 15,743 school districts. Other than tradition, there does not appear to be a rationale for the number of school districts in a single state. For example, Georgia has 185 districts with 1,057,025 students, and Florida has 67 districts with 1,778,494 students. Texas has the largest number of school districts at 1,076, followed by California at 1,012. States with fewer than 100 districts are Alaska, Delaware, Florida, Louisiana, Maryland, Nevada, New Mexico, Rhode Island, South Carolina, Utah, West Virginia, and Wyoming.

The relative ability of a state to support governmental services can be measured in different ways. One measure is the per-capita personal income in the state. As shown in Table 6.7, the 1989 national average per-capita personal income was $17,657. The highest average per-capita personal income was $24,683 in Connecticut, and the lowest was $11,724 in Mississippi.

Since per-capita income generally is recognized as the best single measure of wealth or fiscal ability, the proportion of per-capita income spent for a governmental service such as schools can be used as an indicator of a state's effort. As shown in Table 6.8, in 1988-89 Wyoming had the highest expenditure level for all levels of education at $109 per $1,000 of personal income. Alaska at $105 was the only other state with expenditures of more than $100 per $1,000 of personal income. The national average was $60, and the lowest levels were in Massachusetts and the District of Columbia, both at $45 per $1,000 of personal income.

An alternative indicator of effort for supporting elementary and secondary education is per-capita expenditures by state and local governments. This figure is derived by dividing total expenditures by the total population. However, this figure does not reflect the differences in ability in terms of the per-capita income in a state. As shown in Table 6.9, in 1988-89 the highest per-capita expenditures were in Alaska at $1,700 and in Wyoming at $1,112. The national average per-capita expenditure was $746. The lowest per-capita expenditures were in Tennessee at $502 and Kentucky at $512.

A comparison of the data on per-capita personal income in Table 6.7 with the data on per-capita expenditures in Table 6.9 shows that the high-ability states, as measured by per-capita personal income,

Table 6.6. Average daily attendance and number of districts, 1990-91.

State	ADA	# of Districts
50 States and D.C.	38,099,634	15,473
Alabama	681,865	130
Alaska	95,706	54
Arizona	603,558	217
Arkansas	409,535	324
California	4,978,018	1,012
Colorado	520,859	176
Connecticut	445,500	177
Delaware	92,500	19
District of Columbia	70,548	1
Florida	1,778,494	67
Georgia	1,057,025	185
Hawaii	159,093	1
Idaho	209,798	113
Illinois	1,572,455	959
Indiana	855,945	296
Iowa	454,726	430
Kansas	383,316	304
Kentucky	569,200	176
Louisiana	715,168	66
Maine	198,758	288
Maryland	661,765	24
Massachusetts	771,163	437
Michigan	1,455,735	619
Minnesota	708,973	435
Mississippi	474,109	151
Missouri	730,296	543
Montana	141,628	538
Nebraska	254,811	812
Nevada	170,266	17
New Hampshire	158,903	176
New Jersey	1,006,781	619
New Mexico	254,794	88
New York	2,258,000	720
North Carolina	1,010,040	134
North Dakota	113,000	276
Ohio	1,572,216	613
Oklahoma	542,000	621
Oregon	448,200	300
Pennsylvania	1,504,000	501
Rhode Island	124,440	37
South Carolina	582,351	93
South Dakota	120,205	183
Tennessee	766,337	137
Texas	3,107,760	1,076
Utah	416,229	40
Vermont	88,266	325
Virginia	932,143	137
Washington	784,067	296
West Virginia	297,309	55
Wisconsin	699,480	428
Wyoming	92,300	49

Source: National Education Association, *Estimates of School Statistics, 1990-91* (Washington, D.C., 1991). Table 1, p. 29, and Table 4, p. 32.

Table 6.7. Per-capita personal income by state, 1989.

State	Per Capita Personal Income
Connecticut	$ 24,683
New Jersey	23,778
District of Columbia	23,491
Massachusetts	22,174
Alaska	21,656
New York	21,073
Maryland	21,013
New Hampshire	20,267
California	19,929
Nevada	19,269
Virginia	18,927
Illinois	18,814
Delaware	18,483
Hawaii	18,472
Rhode Island	17,950
Minnesota	17,657
Florida	17,647
Washington	17,657
50 States and D.C. Average	17,596
Colorado	17,553
Michigan	17,444
Pennsylvania	17,269
Kansas	16,498
Wisconsin	16,449
Ohio	16,373
Vermont	16,371
Missouri	16,292
Maine	16,248
Georgia	16,053
Oregon	15,919
Arizona	15,802
Indiana	15,779
Texas	15,702
Iowa	15,487
Nebraska	15,446
North Carolina	15,198
Tennessee	14,694
Wyoming	14,508
Oklahoma	14,154
Montana	14,078
Kentucky	13,743
Idaho	13,707
South Dakota	13,685
South Carolina	13,634
Alabama	13,625
North Dakota	13,563
New Mexico	13,140
Utah	13,079
Louisiana	12,921
Arkansas	12,901
West Virginia	12,354
Mississippi	11,724

Source: Bureau of Economic Analysis, *Survey of Current Business* (August 1990): 28.

Table 6.8. State and local government expenditures for all education in 1988-90 per $1,000 of personal income in 1989.

State	Amount
Wyoming	$ 109
Alaska	105
North Dakota	88
Utah	87
New Mexico	86
Vermont	81
Mississippi	77
Montana	76
Oregon	76
Iowa	75
West Virginia	74
Wisconsin	74
Arizona	73
Nebraska	72
South Carolina	72
Minnesota	71
Delaware	71
Michigan	70
North Carolina	69
Alabama	69
Texas	67
Indiana	67
Oklahoma	67
Maine	66
Arkansas	66
Kansas	66
Louisiana	65
Washington	65
Idaho	65
South Dakota	64
New York	63
Colorado	61
Ohio	61
Georgia	61
Kentucky	61
50 States and D.C. Average	60
Virginia	59
Rhode Island	59
Pennsylvania	58
Tennessee	56
Missouri	55
California	55
Florida	52
Maryland	51
New Jersey	51
New Hampshire	50
Illinois	49
Hawaii	48
Connecticut	47
Nevada	46
District of Columbia	45
Massachusetts	45

Source: National Education Association, *Rankings of the States: 1991* (Washington, D.C., 1991). Table H-4, p. 57.

tend also to be the high-spending states. And the low per-capita personal income states tend to be the low-spending states. However, there are some exceptions to this generalization; a few states with below average per-capita personal income and above average per-capita expenditures are Arizona, Maine, Montana, and Wyoming.

Another measure of a state's effort is the percentage of funds earmarked for all education compared to total state and local general government expenditures. As shown in Table 6.10, the national average in 1989-90 was 34.6%. The highest percentage was in Indiana at 41.9%, followed by Utah at 41.8%, North Carolina at 41.5%, Arkansas at 41.5%, and Vermont at 41.2%. States with the lowest percentages were Alaska at 22.8%, Hawaii at 26.6%, Massachusetts at 27.1%, and New York at 28.6%.

These data include expenditures for all education, not just elementary and secondary schools; but they do provide baseline information about the proportion of state and local governmental expenditures allocated for all education. Therefore, some caution should be exercised in generalizing from these data. For example, a state with a broad array of well-funded governmental services may be spending a smaller proportion of its overall budget for education, even though expenditures may be high in terms of the relationships between effort and ability and in terms of comparisons with other states.

States rank high and low on the different measures. Some of the differences in rankings are attributable to high-wealth (ability) states, which spend more simply because they have this capacity without having to levy high taxes. However, careful analysis of the data will reveal some states that rank high on the different effort measures. This phenomenon may be an indication of the willingness of the citizens to support education.

Federal Funds for Elementary and Secondary Education

Since education is a state responsibility and a local function, the federal government has had a limited role in the financing of elementary and secondary education. Even this limited role has not been without controversy. The general welfare clause in the U.S. Constitution grants to Congress the power to "levy and collect taxes . . . for the common defense and the general welfare of the United States." Congress has interpreted this general welfare clause broadly to justify enactment of legislation and funding for a variety of federal education programs.

Table 6.9. Per-capita expenditures of local and state governments for public elementary and secondary schools, 1988-89.

State	Amount
Alaska	$1,700
Wyoming	1,112
New York	1,030
New Jersey	920
District of Columbia	912
Connecticut	902
Minnesota	863
Oregon	848
Vermont	845
Michigan	827
Wisconsin	807
Montana	788
Washington	786
Arizona	773
Pennsylvania	768
New Hampshire	767
Maine	767
Colorado	767
Virginia	763
Delaware	760
50 States and D.C. Average	746
Maryland	745
Massachusetts	742
California	738
Texas	737
Nebraska	730
Georgia	726
Kansas	721
North Dakota	718
Ohio	718
Iowa	716
New Mexico	709
Indiana	701
Utah	695
Rhode Island	690
Florida	679
North Carolina	671
Missouri	656
Nevada	649
South Carolina	648
Illinois	645
West Virginia	637
South Dakota	635
Oklahoma	634
Louisiana	585
Idaho	582
Mississippi	580
Arkansas	566
Hawaii	544
Alabama	543
Kentucky	512
Tennessee	502

Source: National Education Association, *Rankings of the States: 1991* (Washington, D.C., 1991). Table H-8, p. 58.

Table 6.10. State and local expenditures for all education as
percent of total general expenditures for all functions,
1989-90.

State	% for Education
Indiana	41.9
Utah	41.8
North Carolina	41.5
Arkansas	41.5
Vermont	41.2
Texas	40.8
Nebraska	40.1
South Carolina	39.7
Kansas	39.6
Iowa	39.5
Missouri	39.4
West Virginia	39.2
Alabama	38.7
Wisconsin	38.6
Oregon	38.5
Virginia	38.2
Oklahoma	38.1
Michigan	38.0
Washington	37.9
Mississippi	37.6
New Mexico	37.4
Idaho	37.1
New Hampshire	36.9
North Dakota	36.9
Ohio	36.8
Montana	36.8
Delaware	36.7
Pennsylvania	36.6
Colorado	36.2
Wyoming	35.9
Arizona	35.8
Maine	35.6
South Dakota	35.0
Georgia	34.9
50 States Average	34.6
Illinois	34.2
Tennessee	34.1
Kentucky	33.9
Maryland	33.9
Minnesota	33.7
New Jersey	33.2
Florida	32.2
California	31.8
Rhode Island	31.8
Louisiana	31.2
Connecticut	30.6
Nevada	28.7
New York	28.6
Massachusetts	27.1
Hawaii	26.6
Alaska	22.8

Source: National Education Association, *Rankings of the States: 1991* (Washington, D.C., 1991). Table H-5, p. 57.

Over the years, federal support for elementary and secondary education has continued in a limited way. However, the level of this funding has not kept pace with the increasing costs of education. During the decade of the Eighties, federal funds as a percentage of all funds for elementary and secondary education declined from slightly more than 9% to about 6% (Irwin 1991).

President Reagan entered the White House in 1981 with a pledge to de-emphasize the federal role in education. Secretary of Education Terrel Bell's *A Nation at Risk* report stimulated interest in education but did not result in recommendations for increases in federal funds. Congress, however, had other plans. As shown in Table 6.11, federal funds increased during the decade of the Eighties from $14.5 billion to $27.4 billion. Except for the 1986 fiscal year, the amount of the federal appropriation increased each year. These funds support several traditional federal programs as well as several new ones. The major ones are summarized in the following section.

Throughout its history, the federal education agency has served as a national data collection agency for education. The first major federal education program was enactment of the Smith-Hughes Act in 1917. This early vocational education legislation authorized funds

Table 6.11. Appropriations for the U.S. Department of Education: 1980-1991.

Fiscal Year	Appropriation
1980	$14,477,447,000
1981	14,807,740,000
1982	14,752,370,000
1983	15,422,286,000
1984	15,441,482,000
1985	19,078,624,000
1986	17,939,011,000
1987	19,687,697,000
1988	20,314,175,000
1989	22,738,556,000
1990	24,129,385,000
1991	27,429,582,000

Source: Irwin, P.M., *U.S. Department of Education: Major Program Trends, Fiscal Years 1980-1991*, CRS Report to Congress 91-10 EPW (Washington, D.C.: Congressional Research Service, Library of Congress, 1991), p. 3.

for the salaries of teachers of certain vocational trades, home economics, and industrial subjects. By 1991 federal funding for vocational education exceeded $1 billion annually, but federal funds still
accounted for only about 10% of the total expenditures for vocational
education (Irwin 1991).

The second major program started during World War II was the
Lanham Act, enacted in 1941. This legislation provided local school
districts with extra funds because of the influx of children whose parents worked in defense industries or served in military services at
bases located within the school district. This legislation was continued
with the enactment of the impact aid legislation (Public Laws 81-815
and 81-874) in 1950. Funds still are provided through this legislation. The program provides funds for children of military personnel
and children living with parents who live or work on federal lands,
including federally recognized Indian reservations. In contrast to other
federal programs, impact aid payments are considered to be "in lieu
of local property taxes" and thus may be used for the general operation of schools. By 1991 federal funding for this program was about
$750 million annually (Irwin 1991).

Even though the G.I. Bill did not provide direct funding for elementary and secondary education, the program was a major federal effort to assist in the readjustment of World War II veterans and, later,
Korean War veterans as well. Most would agree that this program
has had a major impact on the nation's economic development. Many
veterans received postsecondary education under this program who,
under ordinary circumstances, would not have had access to these
opportunities. Not only did these better-educated veterans have increased earnings, but they also became a part of the intellectual infrastructure, which contributed to the growth and development of
the nation's economy and to changes in the social system.

The next major federal program was the National Defense Education Act of 1958. This program focused on improvement of instruction in math and science and was a direct response to the Soviet success
in launching Sputnik into space. Funds were provided for the training and retraining of teachers and the purchasing of materials and
equipment to improve instruction in the sciences and mathematics.
Most of the original programs authorized under this legislation have
expired, but it served as a model for some of the later programs funded
under the Elementary and Secondary Education Act of 1965.

Since 1965 the federal role in education has expanded significantly with the enactment of legislation that funded a variety of elemen-

tary and secondary education programs, as well as higher education student-assistance programs. Programs included funds for education of the disadvantaged, instructional materials, local programs to encourage innovation, regional educational research and development centers, and improvement of state education agencies.

Of the continuing federal elementary and secondary education programs, the largest is Chapter 1 for the education of the disadvantaged. The annual funding level for this program in 1991 was about $6.2 billion (Irwin 1991). The intent of the program is to improve educational programs for disadvantaged pupils from low-income homes. These programs are funded completely by the federal government and likely would not be continued if the federal funds were terminated.

Federal funds and regulations for education of handicapped or disabled children under Public Law 94-142 represent a different type of major federal initiative. Under the statute and resulting regulations, local school districts have to provide eligible handicapped or disabled pupils with a free and appropriate education irrespective of the level of federal funds. About 7% of the total school-age population has been classified as handicapped or disabled and in need of special education programs and services. Funds for this program reached about $1.8 billion in 1991 (Irwin 1991). This funding level, coupled with the Chapter 1 funds for the education of disadvantaged pupils, must be put in the context of the total funding of more than $200 billion annually for public elementary and secondary education.

With the increase in federal funding for elementary and secondary education in the Sixties, there also was increased interest in federal funding for educational research. The first major effort along this line was the creation of the National Institute for Education in 1972 under the then U.S. Office of Education. Typically, the actual research was not conducted by federal agencies but was contracted out to universities and private research firms. Currently, federal research funds for education are administered through the Office for Educational Research and Improvement in the Department of Education. With funds from the Department of Education, research, development, and dissemination programs are conducted through regional laboratories and centers. Total federal funds for educational research and statistics in the Department of Education were about $135 million in 1991 (Irwin 1991). However, the total level of federal funding for educational research is difficult to determine because various programs funded under the rubric of research are conducted in a variety of federal agencies, including the National Science Foundation and the Departments of Defense, Labor, and Health and Human Services.

Federal funds also are provided for administering the National Assessment of Educational Progress. This program is designed to provide a general picture of the performance of elementary and secondary pupils in different curriculum areas. State-by-state comparisons are published and have come to be called the "National Report Card." However, since the program tests only a sampling of students in each state, it is not designed to provide performance data on students in a particular district or school.

In 1981 Chapter 2 of the Education Consolidation and Improvement Act combined more than 40 federal categorical educational programs into a block grant to be administered by states and local school districts. Support for the block grant developed because of the proliferation of federal categorical programs. Several smaller targeted programs lost their funding through this consolidation, but funding was retained for education of disadvantaged pupils, education of the handicapped, and vocational education. Increases in federal funds for the Chapter 2 block grants have not kept pace with inflation; overall funding has remained relatively constant since 1981 at about $500 million annually. Funding for 1991 was $484 million (Irwin 1991).

Some observers contend that federal education programs tend to develop in cycles. The Chapter 2 block grant in the Education Consolidation and Improvement Act of 1981 is an example. When the block grant legislation was introduced in 1981, procedures for the competitive discretionary grant programs had become so complex that even program advocates recognized the need for a change. However, with the reauthorization of federal elementary and secondary education programs in 1988, competitive and discretionary federal categorical programs reappeared for special populations, such as at-risk and gifted pupils.

The historical federal role in education can be viewed as a series of efforts to respond to perceived national problems. Examples include improving agriculture and mechanical arts in the 1860s, vocational training after World War I, readjustment problems of veterans after World War II, competition with the Russians in space in the late 1950s, social problems of the nation in the 1960s, and in the 1990s emphasis on maintaining international competitiveness as the nation enters the 21st century.

Over the years, some aspects of the federal role in education have been relatively constant, such as collecting and disseminating national statistical data on all aspects of education. Rather than providing funds for the general support of education, the federal role has typically been to respond to a specific national problem, to fund programs for target populations, and to provide incentives to states and local districts to establish innovative or demonstration programs.

Summary

The principal sources of school revenues continue to be state and local governments, with levels of support varying significantly among the states in both ability and effort. Any resolution of the funding problems schools face ultimately will be made by these entities. The federal proportion of funding has been decreasing, with most funding being targeted for special populations. States and local districts likely will face a slower rate of economic growth, which affects the tax base, and increasing competition for funds from other governmental services.

References

Bureau of the Census. *Government Finances in 1988-89*. GP-90-6. Washington, D.C.: U.S. Government Printing Office, 1990.

Due, J. "Alternative Tax Sources for Education." In *Economic Factors Affecting the Financing of Education*. Gainesville: National Educational Finance Project, University of Florida, 1970.

Irwin, P.M. *U.S. Department of Education: Major Program Trends, Fiscal Years 1980-1991*. CRS Report to Congress 91-10 EPW. Washington, D.C.: Congressional Research Service, Library of Congress, 1991.

National Education Association. *Estimates of School Statistics, 1990-91*. Washington, D.C., 1991.

National Education Association. *Rankings of the States: 1991*. Washington, D.C., 1991.

Robinson, G.E., and Protheroe, N. "Local School Budget Profiles Study." *School Business Affairs* 57 (September 1991): 6-15.

Snyder, T.D. *Digest of Education Statistics*. Washington, D.C.: National Center for Education Statistics, U.S. Department of Education, 1990.

CHAPTER 7

Issues in Public School Finance

The Eighties were characterized by calls for broad-based education reform. Many of the recommendations were additive, calling for increased requirements for graduation, longer school days and years, and higher teacher salaries. Justification for reform reflected the need to improve America's competitiveness in the international economy. However, state legislatures have not provided sufficient funding to implement many of the reform proposals or have failed to fund fully the programs that they have established (Jordan and McKeown 1989). An unintended consequence of the school reform rhetoric may be that it will increase expectations for the schools without providing additional financial resources.

Even as economic growth is slowing at the national and state levels, there are demands for increased funds for such social services as health and welfare, which compete with the funding for education. The unanswered question is whether policymakers will curtail funding for education as the economy slows or will view spending for education as a necessary investment to improve the economic position of the nation and the states.

Several school finance issues face the nation in the decade of the Nineties. They include such diverse concerns as non-tax funding sources for schools, parental choice, student performance as a basis for funding, educational overburden, site-based decision making, incentives for improved school performance, and state-controlled funding systems. Each of these will be discussed in this final chapter.

Non-Tax Sources for School Funds

One of the consequences of tax limitation statutes and of recent litigation seeking greater equity in school funding has been greater reliance on non-tax revenues for funding schools. Even though the proportion of such revenues to the total is small, the policy implications are significant. As the pressures for greater equity increase, several innovative measures have been devised to generate additional funds from non-tax sources. These include student participation fees for school activities, establishment of non-profit educational foundations at the school or district level, and enterprise activities.

Reliance on participation fees as a condition for participating in school activities appears to be in conflict with the principle of equity or equal access to educational programs and services. In some instances, fee waivers are provided for those students unable to pay. Nevertheless, the policy issue is whether such fees are a contradiction of the goal of providing a *free* public education to all students. One consideration is whether the activity is an integral part of the school program or only an adjunct activity under the sponsorship of the school. If the activity is an integral part of the school program, then charging a participation fee would be discriminatory if a poor student is denied access because of inability to pay. As school districts contemplate participation fees, the unanswered question is whether fees will result in lower participation rates for disadvantaged students.

Some school districts and individual schools have created non-profit educational foundations as a way of generating additional income to ensure maintenance of those programs and services that constitute their "margin of quality" or to provide special programs that cannot be supported from tax funds. Such foundations are set up as non-profit organizations (usually with their own board of directors) and are able to receive tax-deductible gifts from parents, other interested citizens, and local businesses. The unanswered question is whether those citizens who support a school's educational foundation also will be supporters of general taxation for funding all schools.

School enterprise activities are designed to secure additional revenues for school operations by undertaking some type of profit-making venture. Such ventures can take different directions. For example, school food service programs and school bookstores can be profit-making ventures with the proceeds being used to supplement regular school funds.

Although resistance by the general public to such ventures might be minimal, local businesses might object because they are in direct competition with them. Also, such ventures might be subject to criticism because they are not related to the primary mission of the pub-

108

lic schools; and any profits could be subject to taxes as unrelated business income. (For higher education institutions, definitions already have been established for unrelated business income activities that are subject to taxation.)

If schools initiate profit-making enterprises, the unanswered question is whether those citizens whose business activities are adversely affected by these ventures will support continued or increased funding for schools.

Parental Choice

One of the outcomes of increased citizen interest in schools is a movement for parents to have a choice in the school their child will attend. One of the earlier choice proposals was to give parents vouchers, paid for by public funds, which they could use to pay for their children's education in a private school. More than 35 years ago, Milton Friedman (1955), the Nobel Prize economist, advocated vouchers as a way to provide parents with choice in the education of their children, as well as a way to subject the public schools to competition in the marketplace. John Coons (1978) has proposed family power equalization as a technique to bring equity into the voucher approach, with the payment per student based on parental income and the number of school-age children in the family. Because of concerns about regulatory controls and about public funds being used for church-related schools, most of the earlier choice proposals were limited to the public schools.

In the late 1980s, the issue of school choice has surfaced again on both the political and educational agendas. As with Friedman's earlier proposal, the assumption is that choice will lead to competition among public schools and that competition will force individual schools to respond to the interests of parents and either improve or close their doors (Chubb and Moe 1990).

By 1991 statutes providing for public school choice or open enrollment plans had been formally adopted or implemented in nine states on both an inter-district and intra-district basis. The plans may be voluntary or mandatory, depending on the authority given school districts to implement a choice program. Ohio and Colorado have mandatory intra-district choice. (The Ohio program does not take effect until the 1993-94 school year.) Iowa, Minnesota, and Nebraska have mandatory inter-district choice plans. Voluntary inter-district and intra-district choice plans are in effect in Arkansas, Idaho, Utah,

109

and Washington. Minnesota was the first state to enact legislation providing for parental choice. Milwaukee is involved in a pilot program that provides vouchers for students to attend non-sectarian private schools in the district (Sheane and Bierlein 1991). In the St. Louis area, as a part of a desegregation agreement, students are permitted to transfer to nearby school districts if such transfers do not promote further segregation.

Choice programs vary considerably, with little consensus about their organizational features and objectives (Riddle and Stedman 1989). Opinions run strong on both sides of the choice issue. Critics of choice maintain that: 1) there is a lack of evidence that choice will improve schools or student performance; 2) youth most in need will be left with the least desirable choices; 3) including private schools could possibly drain funds from needy public schools; and 4) the school's ties with the immediate community may suffer. Proponents contend that choice will contribute to: 1) increased opportunities for poor and minority youth, 2) greater diversity among schools, 3) increased parental interest in schools, and 4) more accountability by schools to improve student performance.

For choice plans to be effective, parents must have sufficient information to make informed choices and must not be unduly influenced by the promotional efforts of a school to attract pupils; all students must have equal access to choice schools, including the child of the working single parent. To enable parents to make informed decisions, they must be provided with comprehensive indicators of good schools that go beyond winning athletic and debate teams, good bands, and high pupil-achievement scores. As states implement parental choice plans, the unanswered question is whether those parents who exercise choice and support their chosen schools also will continue to support increased funding for all schools.

School Funding and Student Performance

Even though much of the school finance litigation has dealt with equity in per-pupil spending, there has been little attention given to outcomes resulting from increased and more equitable funding. Conditions are different in the 1990s. Policymakers now are asking questions about what the money buys, who benefits from the increased funding, and what educational benefits can be traced directly to the increased funds. In a period of reduced economic growth, these questions are important because research does not indicate that more funds necessarily result in better student outcomes (Hanushek 1986). However, some recent findings from the analysis of statewide data in Texas found a positive relationship between teacher literacy and student performance. These findings may encourage additional research into the relationship between inputs and outputs (Ferguson 1991). A recent Educational Testing Service study indicates that a better understanding of the effect of dollars on student performance may be found in an analysis of the resources that actually reach the classroom (Barton et al. 1991).

As pressures for educational reform increase and as more is known about "what works" in schools, legislators may use the state school finance system as an incentive to promote those reforms that have proved successful in terms of improved student performance as well as cost-effectiveness. However, the unanswered question is: What relationship exists between student performance and funding levels?

Educational Overburden

The concept of educational overburden is a complex issue that typically is not addressed in state school finance systems. Educational overburden refers to the additional fiscal burden imposed on a school district because of 1) special conditions requiring higher expenditures per pupil, 2) increased expectations in the form of state mandates without commensurate resources, or 3) greater than expected incidence of special-needs students.

The economic conditions in some school districts are such that a higher per-pupil expenditure is necessary to ensure that all students have equal access to educational programs and services appropriate to their needs. Examples of overburden in urban school districts include campus security costs, transportation to magnet schools, and special schools for at-risk youth. Examples in rural districts include employment incentives such as housing for teachers, higher transportation costs because of population sparsity, and small classes because of low enrollment. The challenge is to quantify the cost elements that contribute to the educational overburden and analyze the effect of including them in a state school finance system.

A second dimension of educational overburden is evident in the school reform movement, such as implementing the National Goals for Education proposed by President Bush and the nation's governors. These reform efforts have resulted in increased expectations from the public. However, as districts attempt to respond to the re-

111

forms, they find that increased funding does not necessarily come with increased expectations. A neglected component in the reform movement has been the failure to make structural changes in state school finance systems to support the reform effort.

The reform mandates may be in the form of state regulations requiring AIDS education, foreign language instruction, ungraded primary, increased graduation requirements, site-based decision making, or a longer school day or year. Some of these may appear to be "no cost" or "low cost" items, but many have "hidden costs" for staff development and organizational changes in the ways that schools operate. Thus school districts are faced with providing additional mandated services with minimal levels of federal and state fiscal support.

Much of the educational overburden related to special-needs students can be attributed to demographic factors (because these students are not uniformly distributed among school districts) and to court decisions. Large urban school districts are enrolling increasing numbers of students with special needs. School districts are under legal mandates to provide adequate funding for these special-needs students, because most of them are in some type of official or unofficial protected class, and their programs have first call on funds. The dilemma is that funds for these mandated programs must be diverted from the regular education program, thus jeopardizing the district's goal of providing a quality and equitable education for all students (Jordan and Lyons 1990).

The courts have failed to address the issue of sufficient funding for special-needs students because of the "absence of judicially manageable standards." As a result, not enough attention has been given to identifying the full range of students with special needs and to ensuring that state funding formulas provide sufficient funds for the educational needs of those special populations. For example, in many instances, only token funding is provided for programs serving at-risk youth and limited-English-proficient students.

Special-needs students are not restricted to poor, low-tax-wealth districts. Many of these students are found in urban and suburban districts with substantial commercial or industrial tax bases. Sometimes these districts have been forced either to "cap" or reduce their spending by court action and the resulting legislation. If the state school finance system provides adequate funding for these special-needs students, then spending caps help to ensure equity. However,

112

if the state system does not provide adequate funding, then the quality of the program for regular students suffers because of the diversion of funds to the special students.

Several conditions will make the goal of providing all students with an educational program appropriate to their needs and aspirations difficult to achieve in the 1990s. Providing adequate funding for education will be difficult because of the declining rate of economic growth and the competition for scarce governmental revenues. The goal of adequacy will be further complicated by the variety of programs and services required to serve the educational needs of an increasingly diverse school population and by the social and legal pressures to provide these students with adequate programs. Legal challenges to current school finance systems and the resulting spending constraints add still another complication to the problem of adequate funding.

As school districts are confronted with educational overburden, the unanswered question is whether state school finance systems can be designed to address the diversity in needs among school districts and whether the equity/reform movement will provide equitable funding or more mandates without commensurate funding.

Site-Based Decision Making

Another recent development in the school reform movement is the push for decentralizing the decision-making process in school districts by empowering staff at the school site. This trend toward decentralization in school districts follows the pattern of management in many businesses. The assumption is that planning and management decisions should be made as closely as possible to where the decisions will be implemented. Thus those responsible for implementing the decisions should have a central role in the decision-making process. An additional assumption is that decentralized decision making will lead to a better understanding and acceptance of district goals and increase the likelihood that they will be attained.

The goal of site-based decision making is to empower school staff and parents by providing them the authority to allocate resources in ways that address the educational needs in their individual school. Site-based decision making does not negate the need for school district goals, objectives, or priorities. Rather, it gives the school staff flexibility in achieving the goals and objectives and addressing the priorities.

113

Complete decentralization in decision making is not possible because individual schools are subject to the policies and regulations of the district; and districts, in turn, are subject to the policies and regulations of the state educational agency. However, there is a growing consensus that schools are more effective and citizen support is greater when school staff have a voice in decisions about their working conditions and the operation of the local school.

Site-based efforts have taken different forms in such large urban areas as Los Angeles, Miami-Dade County (Florida), and New York City, as well as in numerous smaller communities. State legislatures in Kentucky and Texas have mandated full-scale implementation of site-based decision making. Typically, school site councils are formed comprised of teachers, parents, other citizens, and the building principal. Examples of the range of authority and duties of the school site councils may be found in the Kentucky Educational Reform Act of 1990 and in the provisions for the reorganization of the Chicago Public Schools.

Site-based decision making represents a significant departure from traditional ways of operating school districts. Successful implementation requires a rethinking of the ways in which school boards, central office administrators, and school site personnel perceive their roles and relationships and a revision of the decision-making process in school districts.

Successful implementation of site-based decision making involves developing a detailed district implementation plan. This is usually done by a committee appointed by the school board. Typically, the committee includes school board members, central office administrators, building principals, teachers, support staff, and citizens. This plan establishes the authority limits for local school councils on such matters as school operations, budgets, hiring and dismissal of personnel, and local programming. Prior to implementation of the plan, it is critical that all involved receive a comprehensive orientation to the plan. Also, continuing technical assistance must be available to school site and central office staff.

Even with a well-conceived and carefully implemented plan, problems may emerge. One potential problem is that this power sharing will lead to excessive diversity among schools in a district. Another is that site administrators may be unwilling to involve staff and citizens as full participants in the decision-making process. A third is that some site unit administrators may not have the skills required for successful implementation of site-based decision making.

114

As school districts move toward site-based decision making, the unanswered questions are what effect this change will have on the governance structure for public education and whether this new structure will be able to respond to state mandates for educational accountability.

Financial Incentives for Outstanding School Performance

For several years the U.S. Department of Education has conducted a school recognition program drawing attention to those schools with high student achievement and overall excellence. Such schools are designated as Merit Schools. President Bush's America 2000 Program also has emphasized recognition of exemplary schools (U.S. Department of Education 1991). The Merit Schools concept also is consistent with the emphasis on student achievement in the National Goals for Education.

An extension of the Merit School recognition program might be developed that would provide incentive funds based on criteria that were broader than just student achievement. For example, a program could be developed that provided incentive funds recognizing three categories of schools: 1) those that had high student performance, 2) those that are improving, and 3) those whose performance exceeded expectations. Kentucky and Texas have enacted school recognition programs that do provide financial incentives.

Using statewide achievement test results, all schools could be ranked on the basis of their student performance, ranked on the basis of improved student achievement from the prior year, and ranked on the extent to which student performances exceeded expectations. In the latter category, variables that might be taken into consideration in the comparison of actual performance with expected or predicted performance include students on free and reduced-price lunch, non-English-speaking students, students in Chapter 1 programs, students scoring below the average on normed achievement tests, student mobility, ratio of discipline referrals to number of students, and drop-out rate.

If all three categories were to be recognized, a formula could be set up that awarded incentive funds to 10% of the schools in the state in each category. Thus 30% of the schools in the state would be recognized with incentive funds. Incentive funds for each qualifying school might be set at 1% of the state or national average per-pupil expenditure times the school's enrollment. The total cost of the program would be only 0.3% of the total expenditures for elementary and secondary schools in a state. This small investment in state funds could be sufficient incentive for significant changes in the schools. If the program became too cumbersome to administer or did not seem to work, it could be terminated after two or three years without great harm to the regular school program.

Consistent with site-based decision making, an individual school committee could determine how to use the incentive funds. Constraints might be placed on the use of funds, such as no salary supplements or bonuses for teachers. However, the school committee would have the authority to spend the funds for any other legitimate purpose, such as supplies, library books, videotapes, curriculum consultants, or attendance at professional conferences.

In using incentives as a supplemental funding mechanism, the unanswered questions are whether such incentives will have a positive effect on all schools and what action should be taken in those schools where student performance does not improve or declines.

State-Controlled Full-Funding Systems

In an era of judicial and policy reform in education, many feel that the state should fulfill its responsibility by assuming total funding of public education. If this were to happen, it would represent a dramatic change from the traditional system of the state and local districts sharing in the financing and governance of public education.

Proponents of such a change contend that it would provide greater equity for both students and taxpayers. Although some variation in expenditures would be permitted, it would not be related to disparities in local taxable wealth, which have been the target of a series of court cases. Under a state full-funding system, debate will continue over whether funding limits should be placed on the formerly high-spending districts with high taxable wealth. In many of these districts, the funds to meet local aspirations could be raised with modest tax rates because of high taxable wealth, thus allowing these districts to spend more per pupil with lower tax rates than low-wealth districts could spend.

At the same time as reform proposals are being made for full-state funding of public education, other reform efforts are directed at decentralization, deregulation, teacher empowerment, parental involvement, site-based accountability, and improved student performance. Reconciling these often contradictory reform efforts is possibly the greatest challenge confronting education policymakers in the 1990s. Their task will be to conceptualize and implement a decentralized management system that is compatible with a centralized accountability and funding system.

Under a full-state funding system that ensures that all students have equal access to an adequate education, the first responsibility will be to provide an adequate base level of funding for all students. Then, the state system will have to fully recognize the complete range of special-needs students and their relative cost differences, as well as recognize all uncontrollable variations in expenditures among school districts. If the state system does not meet these responsibilities, local districts should have taxing authority as an escape valve to secure additional funding. If funding is insufficient and expenditures/revenues are controlled by the state, then the state system will constrain school districts in addressing the educational needs of their youth. Such controls would be most unfair to districts with large percentages of special-needs students and other unique conditions that increase the costs of education.

From a public policy perspective, implementation of a state system will require a change in the traditional practices used to develop state budgets for the public schools. In the traditional system where schools were funded from combined state and local revenues, legislatures could reduce state funds knowing that local funds could fill the gap. When the judicial and public policy reforms are coupled with a reduced economic growth and competing demands from other governmental services, state controls on funding public education could lead to reductions in educational programs. Local districts would no longer have the option of securing relief by raising local taxes to address those needs that were not recognized in the state finance system or to replace lost state funds.

If a state full-funding system is to become a reality, the funding formula must have sufficient flexibility to recognize and fund the diversities in educational and operational conditions among school districts. Given the inadequacies of current research to identify and quantify variations in program costs among students and school districts, attaining educational equity through a comprehensive state funding system for public education remains a distant goal.

The concept of a state full-funding system for schools is appealing because it appears to satisfy the requirements of equity. But, in practice, it could result in unfair treatment for students, because there

117

currently are no generally accepted methods of identifying the full range of legitimate cost differences among educational programs and districts. Without such methods, the state funding systems might fail to recognize many high-cost items.

In addition, there are no agreed-on standards as to what should be included in a state system or how the system should work. This problem is illustrated in the following section of the Kentucky Education Reform Act of 1990, which was enacted in response to a ruling by that state's supreme court that the entire Kentucky school system was unconstitutional:

> In determining the cost of the program to support educational excellence in Kentucky, the statewide guaranteed base funding level . . . shall be computed by dividing the amount appropriated for this purpose by the prior year's statewide average daily attendance. (House Bill 940, 1990)

Thus the per-pupil amount required for "educational excellence" is not based on any research on the cost variations for different groups of students or different conditions in districts; rather, it is determined by "dividing the amount appropriated . . . by the year's average daily attendance."

As the legislative and regulatory policy decisions concerning this state system are implemented, the unanswered questions are whether state funds for public education will 1) be based on educational needs and have enough flexibility to encourage diversity that contributes to improvement, or 2) be the product of interacting political and economic conditions that result in a standard delivery system for education that resembles the state system used for mental health, prisons, and highways.

Unintended Consequences

Among the various education reform groups, the single point of agreement appears to be dissatisfaction with the current school finance system and the need for significant change. Without careful consideration of all the interacting factors, "change for the sake of change" may have several unintended consequences, some of which are listed below.

1. Expenditures for education may be perceived as a budget item that can be curtailed as the economy slows rather than as a necessary investment to improve the nation's or state's economic position.

118

2. Fees for student participation in school activities may result in reduced access for disadvantaged students.
3. A decline in tax revenues for schools and greater inequities in per-pupil spending may occur because of the perceived availability of non-tax revenues for schools through educational foundations and profit-making ventures.
4. Parental choice may result in a dual system with some schools attended by students whose parents "care" about education and other schools attended by students whose parents "do not care" about education, with a potential financial advantage accruing to those schools in which the parents "care."
5. Parental choice may lead to a funding system of vouchers for both public and private schools, with the possibility of the public schools becoming "pauper" schools because of the ability of some parents to supplement the vouchers.
6. A levelling of expenditures for public schools may result because of the constraints imposed by school finance equity legislation.
7. Increased mandates and extensive accountability requirements from the state may conflict with the current emphasis on decentralization, deregulation, and teacher empowerment.
8. The emergence of a series of schools without common goals, the dismantling of traditional school governance structures, the disruption of educational service delivery systems, and lack of accountability may occur as a result of decentralization and site-based decision making.
9. A decline in citizen support for public schools may occur because of the diversion of funds from programs and services for the regular child to programs and services for special populations.
10. Incentive programs for school improvement may result in standardization rather than diversity among schools, increased state intervention rather than technical assistance, and a loss of public confidence and support for the low-performing schools that receive no recognition.

State school finance systems are increasingly affected by a series of interactive and non-complementary developments, such as parental choice, educational overburden, equity litigation, decentralization, slowing rate of economic growth, and inadequate funding for special populations. These developments raise a variety of public policy concerns about the future of public education in general, and school finance in particular. One is whether traditional governance structures and financing systems for public education are sufficiently resilient to accommodate the magnitude of change proposed by the education reformers. Another concern is whether the citizen commitment to public education is sufficient to generate political support for the taxes required to fund adequate educational programs for all youth. A final concern is whether the effect of judicial and public policy reforms, combined with the quest for attaining the National Goals for Education, will lead to state or federal legislation providing public funds or vouchers for private schools, thus diverting scarce funds from public schools.

These concerns illustrate the diverse challenges confronting public education. They present an opportunity to restructure the educational delivery system and involve citizens and professional educators in educational decision making. The education profession has the opportunity to provide the leadership in this reform effort and to revive the vision of the schools as an essential element in the American culture. As public education demonstrates the capacity to respond to these challenges, the degree of public confidence will be evidenced by the willingness to provide sufficient funding. This willingness will be determined by the degree to which parents, the general citizenry, and decision makers perceive that the schools are responsive and effective.

References

Barton, P.E.; Coley, R.J.; and Goertz, M.E. *The State of Inequality*. Princeton, N.J.: Educational Testing Service, 1991.

Chubb, J.E., and Moe, T.M. *Politics, Markets, and America's Schools*. Washington, D.C.: Brookings Institution, 1990.

Coons, J.E., and Sugarman, S.D. *Education by Choice*. Berkeley: University of California Press, 1978.

Ferguson, R.F. "Paying for Public Education: New Evidence on How and Why Money Matters." *Harvard Journal on Legislation* 28 (Summer 1991): 465-98.

Friedman, M. "The Role of Government in Education." In *Economics and the Public Interest*, edited by R.A. Solo. New Brunswick, N.J.: Rutgers University Press, 1955.

Hanushek, E.A. "The Economics of Schooling." *Journal of Economic Literature* 24 (1986): 1141-77.

House Bill 940, Kentucky Educational Reform Act. Frankfort: Kentucky General Assembly, 1990.

Jordan, K.F., and Lyons, T.S. "Improving the Equity and Funding Adequacy of the Arizona School Finance Program." Research report. Phoenix, Ariz.: Phoenix Union High School District, 1990.

Jordan, K.F., and McKeown, M.P. "State Fiscal Policy and Education Reform." In *The Educational Reform Movement of the 1980s: Perspectives and Cases*, edited by J. Murphy. Berkeley, Calif.: McCutchan, 1989.

Riddle, W., and Stedman, J.B. *Public School Choice: Recent Developments and Analysis of Issues.* CRS Report to Congress 89-219 EPW. Washington, D.C.: Congressional Research Service, Library of Congress, 1989.

Sheane, K., and Bierlein, L. *Open Enrollment/Educational Choice.* Tempe: Morrison Institute for Public Policy, School of Public Affairs, Arizona State University, 1991.

U.S. Department of Education. *America 2000: An Education Strategy.* Washington, D.C., 1991.